THE WHITE-HAIRED GIRL

STALIN PRIZE OPERA
1951

THE WHITE-HAIRED GIRL

An Opera in Five Acts

by

Ho Ching-chih and Ting Yi

Foreign Languages Press
Peking 1954

First Edition . . . . January 1954

TRANSLATED BY
YANG HSIEN-YI and GLADYS YANG

Printed in the People's Republic of China

HOW "THE WHITE-HAIRED GIRL" WAS WRITTEN AND PRODUCED

Ho Ching-chih

In 1940, in northwest Hopei, which was part of the Border Region,[1] there spread a story about a "white-haired goddess." Owing to the deep-rooted super-stition of the villagers and cadres of a certain village near the mountains, our work there had made little progress even though several years had passed since the place was liberated by the Eighth Route Army. Rumour had it that a "white-haired goddess" had appeared. She was said to be all in white, and to reveal herself at night. This deity had made the temple just outside the village her dwelling place, and ordered the villagers to sacrifice to her twice a month. For a long time her command was obeyed and, strange to relate, the sacrifice set out one evening always dis-appeared by the following morning. Once, however, when the villagers neglected to place offerings there at the appointed time, a shrill, strange voice sounded from the dark shrine:

"You who neglect your goddess—beware!"

One day a cadre from the district administration office went to the village and fixed a date for a general meeting to elect village officers. When the day came,

---

[1] Referring to the liberated areas bordering on Shansi, Chahar and Hopei provinces.

however, the villagers failed to attend; and when asked the reason the village cadres explained diffidently:

"Today there's a full moon; they've all gone to sacrifice to the 'White-haired Goddess.' "

After ascertaining details, the district cadre decided either the villagers must have mistaken some wild animal for a goddess, or this was some enemy scheme of sabotage. He determined to go to the temple to lay this ghost. That same evening he and the village security officer went, armed, to the temple and hid themselves in a dark corner west of the shrine. After midnight, when the worshippers had left and the moon was shining fitfully, there came a gust of cold wind and footsteps were heard. Then a white figure entered the temple. In the dim light it was just possible to see it snatching food from the altar. As it turned to leave, the district cadre leapt out from his hiding place, and shouted:

"What are you?"

Startled, the apparition gave a wild shriek, then rushed at him. The cadre fired, and it fell, only to struggle at once to its feet and make hastily off. The two men pursued the white figure through the woods and up the mountain until, after passing several cliffs, they lost sight of it. They were standing there irresolutely when they heard a child crying in the distance, and peering through the darkness saw a mysterious flicker of light at the end of the dark mountain gully. Pressing on boldly they discovered a deep, dark cave, in the recesses of which the "White-haired Goddess" was shrinking, clasping a child. The cadre covered her with his gun, and said:

"What are you? Speak up, and I'll spare your life! Otherwise I'll fire!"

The "White-haired Goddess" dropped to her knees before the cadres, crying bitterly, then poured out her story.

Nine years earlier (before the War of Resistance to Japanese Aggression broke out and before the Eighth Route Army reached this district), there had been a wicked landlord in the village, who oppressed the peasants cruelly. One of his old tenants had a daughter of seventeen, an intelligent and pretty girl who took his fancy; so on the pretext of collecting rent he contrived to drive her father to commit suicide, then carried off the girl, and when he had her in his clutches raped her. Later she became pregnant. When this happened, he decided to murder her and take a new wife, but his plot was discovered by a kind-hearted maidservant, who helped the girl to escape by night. However, after flying from the landlord's house she had nowhere to go; so she found a mountain cave in which to stay, and there she had a child.

Nursing her hatred and bitterness, she remained several years in the cave. Because she went cold and hungry, was seldom in the sun, and had no salt in her diet, her hair turned white. Villagers who saw her stealing offerings from the temple thought her a goddess, and sacrificed to her. So she was able to keep alive. She knew nothing of the war or liberation by the Eighth Route Army, quite unaware that the world had changed.

The girl's story brought the old, evil, man-devouring society before the cadre's eyes, and he was moved to tears. He explained to the "White-haired Goddess" the changes that had taken place since the Eighth Route Army liberated the people, and that tragedies like hers were things of the past, for now the people had become masters of their own destiny and were leading a happier life than ever before. Finally, he brought her out of the dark cave into the bright sunlight. Once more she became a human being, and started a new life.

This story was told and retold. It was amended, amplified and polished by the people. From the first day of telling, it spread rapidly, and soon enjoyed immense popularity. Writers of the Border Region wrote it up into short stories, songs and reportage, and by 1944 it had reached Yenan.

As with all stories handed down orally, there were different versions, and ours is only one of many. However, the variants differ only in certain episodes: the central theme, chief characteristics and main episodes are common to all. When we hear this story we are deeply moved by it, for it is a superb folk tale. Through the tragic experiences of the daughter of a tenant peasant, it gives concentrated expression to the sufferings of the peasants under the dark feudal rule of old China, at the same time revealing the splendour of new China and the new democracy led by the Communist Party in which the peasants have become their own masters. In the words of the opera: "The old society changed men into ghosts, while the new society changes ghosts into men." Such a folk tale came into circulation in the Border Region mainly because after centuries of hardship the Chinese peasants had been liberated. Under the leadership of the Communist Party their life has undergone a radical change, and light has flooded their hearts, stimulating their imaginations and intelligence. Thus this story is endued with actual, positive significance and the revolutionary romanticism of the people's struggle.

The libretto adopted the central theme of the folk story, and retained some of its chief characteristics and episodes. However, in order to bring out the main theme clearly and forcefully and adapt it for effective stage representation, certain alterations were made to the original story.

It took some time to understand and portray the main theme. To begin with it was considered by some as a ghost story devoid of any social significance. Others felt it could be written up as a story to overcome superstition. Later, however, after careful study, we came to consider it not merely as a ghost story or an attack upon superstition but grasped its more positive aspect—the portrayal of the contrast between the two types of society and the significance of the people's liberation.

Writing the libretto and rehearsing took more than three months (January—April 1945), during which time we never ceased experimenting and revising. We lacked experience in writing, and knew too little about life in the Border Region; above all we were ill-equipped to handle the opera form and technique. We asked advice from comrades familiar with that region, at the same time making use of our past experience in rural work; and we consulted many friends about the episodes of the story while writing the libretto. During rehearsals the libretto was revised by the performers and producer, and many experts and students offered good advice. Particularly noteworthy is the fact that many of the country folk, as well as our school messengers and cooks, came eagerly to watch the rehearsals and made excellent suggestions, even on very minor points. When we wrote the last act describing the new society, we also asked the advice of comrades engaged in administrative work in the Border Region.

In April 1945, the opera was produced in Yenan. More than thirty performances were given in all, and it was very well received. Most of our cadres and the local people came to see it, some even from a considerable distance. The songs became well known, and in the street members of our cast were often pointed out.

"That's the white-haired girl!" someone would say.

"There's Tenant Yang!"

And sometimes children gathered to point their fingers at us and say mischievously:

"The running-dog Mu is here!"

"Landlord Huang, you bad egg!"

"It's all true to life," said country folk discussing the story. "We've all come from the old society. Who wouldn't cry at the dreadful things that happened to that girl!"

One labour hero who saw the opera was reminded of the past when he had been forced to sell his daughter. "I shall never forget!" he said. "Today with the Communists guiding us, we poor people have really become masters."

One characteristic of the cultural life of Yenan was the special attention paid to drama and the enthusiastic criticism given both by cadres and the masses. This being the case, *The White-haired Girl* was constantly revised as a result of suggestions and criticisms received. When we sat with the audience to watch performances, or listened to their comments afterwards, we often heard the most unrestrained, genuine and valuable comments. Sometimes we also solicited the opinion of play-goers, both cadres and ordinary citizens.

In October 1945, we went to Kalgan where we decided to produce *The White-haired Girl* again. We received great assistance from the comrades engaged in literary work there, who were familiar with local conditions and had rich working experience. Thanks to their advice, and bearing in mind the criticism of previous audiences, we made further changes in the libretto. Important revisions were made also in 1947, and again in 1949 when we wrote the final version of the opera.

The foregoing account of the composition of the opera makes it clear that this is a collective work with a wide mass basis and a new significance. The libretto, for instance, is based on a folk tale founded on real life which was already the work of many people. Then the opera was studied, criticized and revised by many others, who assisted directly or indirectly in its making. Without collective effort and co-operation, *The White-haired Girl* could never have come into being.

Most important is the fact that, apart from assistance received from experts, artists and cadres, this opera was composed mainly by means of the help and criticism of the masses. The people are our teachers, and it was they who taught us how to work. They are our most reliable judges and authoritative critics. The new art serves the masses and reflects their lives, and the masses are the characters and the critics, sometimes the creators too, of this art, as our experience proves.

CONTENTS

CHARACTERS

YANG *tenant of Landlord Huang, aged over fifty.*

HSI-ERH *Yang's daughter, aged seventeen.*

AUNTY WANG *Yang's neighbour, a peasant woman of over fifty.*

TA-CHUN *Aunty Wang's son, about twenty.*

UNCLE CHAO *Yang's old friend, a tenant peasant of about fifty.*

LI *a peasant, over forty.*

TA-SO *a young peasant.*

HUANG *a landlord in his thirties.*

MRS. HUANG *Landlord Huang's mother, over fifty.*

MU *the Huang family steward, in his thirties.*

AUNTY CHANG *a servant in the Huang family, in her forties.*

TA-SHENG *a servant in the Huang family, in his twenties.*

TWO THUGS EMPLOYED BY THE HUANG FAMILY.

THE DISTRICT HEAD.

HU-TZU *a young peasant.*

FOUR PEASANTS.

FOUR PEASANT WOMEN.

CROWD.

ACT I

TIME   *Winter, 1935.*

PLACE   *Yangko Village in Hopei. There is a plain before the village, and hills behind.*

SCENE   I   *New Year's Eve in the home of the tenant peasant Yang.*

SCENE II   *A room beside the reception hall of the Huang house that same evening.*

            The entrance to the Huang house.

SCENE III   *The road to the village, that same evening. Yang's home.*

SCENE IV   *In front of Yang's home the next day.*

ACT II

SCENE   I   *Mrs. Huang's Buddhist shrine on New Year's morning.*

SCENE II   *In front of Aunty Wang's house, a month later.*

            In front of Uncle Chao's house.

SCENE III   *An evening several days later in the Huang house.*

            Mrs. Huang's bedroom.
            The entrance to Landlord Huang's study.
            Landlord Huang's study.

SCENE IV   *The next morning in the Huang house. Landlord Huang's study.*

ACT III

ACT IV

ACT V

ACT I

TIME   *Winter, 1935.*

PLACE   *Yangko Village in Hopei.   There is a plain in
front of the village, and hills behind.*

SCENE I

It is New Year's Eve, and heavy snow is falling.
HSI-ERH, *daughter of the tenant peasant* YANG, *comes
on through the snowstorm carrying maize flour.*

HSI-ERH (*sings*):
> The north wind blows, the snow flakes whirl,
> A flurry of snow brings in New Year.
> Dad's been hiding a week because of his debt,
> Though it's New Year's Eve, he's still not back.
> Aunty's given me maize flour, and I'm waiting
> For Dad to come home and spend New Year.
> (*Pushing open the door, she goes in.   It is a hum-
> ble room, containing a stove with a kitchen-god
> beside it and firewood and pots stacked in one corner.
> On the stove stands an oil lamp.*)

HSI-ERH   Now it's New Year's Eve, everybody's
steaming maize cakes and dumplings, burning incense and pasting up door-gods for New Year.   Dad
has been away for a week, and still isn't back.   We've
nothing in the house for New Year.   (*Pauses.*)
There are only Dad and I at home: my mother died

when I was three. My father cultivates one acre of land belonging to rich Landlord Huang. Dad works in the fields with me at his heels, in the wind and in the rain....Every year we're behind with our rent, so just before New Year he always leaves home to escape being dunned. (*Anxiously.*) Now it's New Year's Eve, and getting quite dark—why isn't he back yet? Oh, I went to Aunty's house just now, and she gave me some maize flour which I'm going to mix with bean cake to make cakes for Dad to eat when he comes back. (*She fetches water, mixes the dough and starts making cakes.*)

(*The wind blows open the door.* HSI-ERH *runs over, but finds no one there.*)

HSI-ERH Oh, it's the wind that blew open the door. (*Sings*) :
Wind whirls the snow against our door,
Wind batters the door till it flies wide open.
I'm waiting for Dad to come back home,
And step inside the room again!

When Dad left, he took beancurd to sell. If he's sold the beancurd and brings back two pounds of flour, we could even eat dumplings. (*Sings*) :
I feel so restless waiting for Dad,
But when he comes home I'll be happy.
He'll bring some white flour back with him,
And we'll have a really happy New Year!
(*She continues making cakes.*)

(*Enter* YANG *covered with snow. He has his pedlar's pole and kit for carrying beancurd, and over his shoulders the cloth used to cover the beancurd. He staggers along.*)

YANG (*sings*) :
Three miles through a snowstorm I've come home,
After hiding a week from the duns.
As long as I can get by this time,

I don't mind putting up with hunger and cold.
(*After looking round apprehensively he knocks at the door.*) Hsi-erh! Open the door!
(HSI-ERH, *overjoyed, opens the door.*)

HSI-ERH You're back, Dad!

YANG Yes. (*He signs to her not to talk so loudly.*)

HSI-ERH (*brushing the snow from her father's clothes*) It's snowing very hard outside, Dad! Look how thickly you're covered!

YANG While I was away, Hsi-erh, did the landlord send anyone to press for payment?

HSI-ERH On the 25th, Steward Mu came.

YANG (*taken aback*) Oh? He came? What did he say?

HSI-ERH When he found you were away he left again.

YANG And then?

HSI-ERH He hasn't been back since.

YANG (*rather incredulous*) Really?

HSI-ERH Yes, Dad.

YANG (*still unconvinced*) Are you sure?

HSI-ERH Why should I fool you, Dad?

YANG (*reassured*) Well, that's good. Listen, Hsi-erh, how strong the wind is!

HSI-ERH And it's snowing so hard!

YANG It's growing dark too.

HSI-ERH And the road is bad, Dad.

YANG I don't think Steward Mu will come now. I owe the landlord one and a half piculs, and my debt with the interest amounts to twenty-five dollars; but this time I've got by.

HSI-ERH (*happily*) So we've got by again, Dad!

YANG Hsi-erh, fetch some firewood so that I can dry myself. Have you still not finished that maize flour?

HSI-ERH I finished that long ago. This is some Aunty Wang gave me just now.

YANG So you've been to the mountain for firewood again in such cold.

HSI-ERH I went just now with Ta-chun. (*She fetches firewood.*) You must be hungry, Dad.

YANG (*warming himself by the fire*) I'm hungry all right. (*Chuckles.*)

HSI-ERH The cakes are mixed, I'm going to steam them.

YANG Just a minute, Hsi-erh. What do you think this is? (*Producing a wallet from his pocket.*)

HSI-ERH (*clutching at it in delighted surprise*) What is it, Dad?

YANG (*sings*):
>With the money I made by selling beancurd,
>I bought two pounds of flour at the fair;
>But I didn't want Landlord Huang to see it,
>So it's been in my wallet the last few days.

HSI-ERH (*sings*):
>With the money he made by selling beancurd,
>Dad bought two pounds of flour at the fair.
>He's brought it home to make dumplings,
>So now we'll have a happy New Year!

Dad, I'll call Aunty Wang over to make dumplings.

YANG (*stopping her*) Wait a bit, Hsi-erh! Look what this is.

HSI-ERH What, Dad?

YANG (*takes a thickly wrapped paper packet from his pocket. When all the paper wrappings are removed, a red ribbon is disclosed. While taking off the wrappings, he sings*):
>Other girls have flowers to wear,
>But your dad can't afford to buy flowers;
>So I bought two feet of red ribbon
>To tie in my Hsi-erh's hair!

(HSI-ERH *kneels before* YANG *who ties the ribbon in her hair.*)

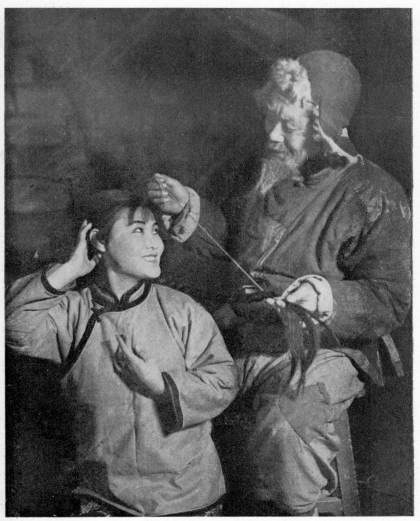

"So I bought two feet of red ribbon
To tie in my Hsi-erh's hair!"

HSI-ERH (*sings*):
> *Other girls have flowers to wear,*
> *But Dad can't afford to buy flowers;*
> *So he's bought two feet of red ribbon*
> *For me to tie in my hair!*
>
> (HSI-ERH *stands up.*)

YANG (*laughs*) Turn round and let me have a look at you. (HSI-ERH *turns.*) Good. Presently we'll ask Ta-chun and Aunty Wang to come and have a look too. (HSI-ERH *tosses her head shyly yet coquettishly.*) Oh, I brought two door-gods too. Let's paste them up. (*He takes out two pictures.*)

HSI-ERH Door-gods! (*They paste them up and sing*):
> *The door-gods ride roan horses!*

YANG:
> *Pasted on the door they'll guard our home!*

HSI-ERH:
> *The door-gods carry such big swords!*

YANG:
> *They'll keep out all devils, great and small!*

BOTH:
> *They'll keep out all devils, great and small!*

YANG Aha, now neither big devils nor little devils can get in!

HSI-ERH I hope that rent-collector, Steward Mu, will be kept out too!

YANG Good girl, let's hope we have a peaceful New Year.

> (*They close the door.*)
>
> (*Enter* AUNTY WANG *from next door.*)

WANG Today Ta-chun bought two pounds of flour at the fair. I'm going to see if Uncle Yang has come back or not, and if he's back I'll ask them over to eat dumplings. (*Looks up.*) Ah, Uncle Yang must be back: the door-gods are up. (*Knocks.*) Hsi-erh! Open the door!

HSI-ERH   Who is it?

WANG   Your aunty.

HSI-ERH   (*opens the door and* WANG *enters*)   See, Aunty, Dad's back!

WANG   How long have you been back, Uncle Yang?

YANG   Just the time it takes to smoke one pipe.

HSI-ERH   Aunty, Dad's bought two pounds of flour. I was just going to ask you over to make dumplings, and now here you are.   Look, look!

WANG   Ta-chun has bought two pounds of flour too, child, and for half a pint of rice he got a pound of pork as well.   I was going to ask you both to our home.

HSI-ERH   Have them over here!

WANG   No, come on over.

HSI-ERH   Do stay here, Aunty!

YANG   Yes, stay here.

WANG   Look at you both!   Why stand on ceremony with us!   (*Turns and whispers to* YANG.)   Uncle, after New Year Hsi-erh and Ta-chun will be one year older.   I'm waiting for you to say the word!

YANG (*afraid lest* HSI-ERH *hear, yet apparently eager for her to hear*)   Don't be impatient, Aunty.   When the right time comes we'll fix it up for the youngsters.   Ah....

HSI-ERH (*pretending not to understand, interrupts them*)   Aunty, come and mix the dough.

YANG   That's right: go and mix the dough.

(AUNTY, *chuckling, goes to mix dough.*)

(*Enter the landlord's steward,* MU. *He carries a lantern bearing the words, "The Huang Family —House of Accumulated Virtue."*)

MU (*sings*):

Here I come collecting rent
And dunning for debt!
I've four treasures as tricks of the trade:

Incense and a gun,
Crutches and a bag of tricks.
I burn the incense before the landlord,
I fire the gun to frighten tenants,
With my crutches I trip folk up,
And with my bag of tricks I cheat them!

This evening the landlord has sent me on an errand to the tenant peasant Yang—a secret errand, not for everybody's ears! The landlord has given me instructions to take Yang to him for a talk. (*Knocks.*) Old Yang, open up!

YANG Who is it?

MU I, Steward Mu!

(*The three inside start, and* AUNTY WANG *and* HSI-ERH *hastily hide the flour bowl.*)

MU Old Yang, hurry up, and let me in!

(*There is no help for it but to open the door, and* MU *enters. All remain silent.*)

MU (*makes a round of the room with his lantern.* HSI-ERH *hides behind* AUNTY WANG) Old Yang! (*With unusual politeness.*) Are you ready for New Year?

YANG Oh, Mr. Mu, we haven't lit the stove yet.

MU Well, Old Yang, I have to trouble you. Landlord Huang wants you to come over for a talk.

YANG Oh! (*Greatly taken aback.*) But... but... Mr. Mu, I can't pay the rent or the debt.

MU Oh no, this time Landlord Huang doesn't want to see you either about the rent or your debt, but to discuss something important. It's New Year's Eve, and the landlord is in a good humour, so you can talk things over comfortably. Come along!

YANG (*pleadingly*) I... Mr. Mu....

MU (*pointing to the door*) It's all right. Come along. (YANG *has to go.*)

HSI-ERH (*hastily*) Dad, you....

MU (*shining the lantern on* HSI-ERH'S *face*) Oh, don't worry, Hsi-erh. Landlord Huang will give you flowers to wear. Your dad will bring them back. (*Laughs.*)

WANG (*putting the beancurd cloth over* YANG'S *shoulders*) Put this over you, Uncle! The snow is heavier now.... When you get there, go down on your knees to Landlord Huang, and he surely won't spoil our New Year.

MU That's right. (*Pushes* YANG *out.*)

(YANG *looks back as he goes out.*)

HSI-ERH Dad!...

(YANG *sighs.*)

MU Hurry up! (*Pushes* YANG *off.*)

HSI-ERH Aunty, my dad!... (*Cries.*)

WANG (*putting her arms round her*) Your dad will be back soon. Come on, come to our house to mix dough.

(*They go out.*)

(*CURTAIN*)

SCENE II

LANDLORD HUANG'S *house.*

The stage presents the entrance and a small room near the reception hall, furnished with a table and chairs. The candle in a tall candlestick on the table lights up an account book, abacus, inkstone and old-fashioned Chinese pipe.

Sounds of laughter, clinking of wine-cups and the shouts of guests playing the finger-game are heard offstage. LANDLORD HUANG *comes in, cheerfully tipsy, picking his teeth.*

HUANG (*sings*):
> *With feasting and wine we see the Old Year out,*
> *And hang lanterns and garlands to celebrate*
> *   New Year's Eve!*
> *There are smiles on the faces of all our guests*
> *Who are drunk with joy, not wine.*
> *Our barns are bursting with grain,*
> *So who cares if the poor go hungry!*
> (*The servant* TA-SHENG *brings in water, and* HUANG *rinses his mouth.*)

HUANG   Ta-sheng, go and tell your mistress I have a headache and can't drink with the guests. Ask her to entertain them.

TA-SHENG   Very good, sir. (*Exit.*)

HUANG   Well, I haven't lived in vain! I have nearly a hundred hectares of good land, and every year I collect at least a thousand piculs in rent. All my life I've known how to weight the scales in my own favour and manage things smoothly both at home and outside. During the last few years our family has done pretty well. Last year my wife died. My mother wants me to marry again, but I feel freer without a wife at home. Women are cheap as dirt. If one takes my fancy, like this one tonight, it's very easy to arrange.

> (MU *leads* YANG *on.*)

YANG (*sings timidly*):
> *The red lanterns under the eaves dazzle my eyes,*
> *And I don't feel easy in my mind.*
> *I wonder what he wants me for?*
> *Hsi-erh is waiting for me at home.*

MU   Old Yang, Landlord Huang is here. This way. (*They enter the room.*)

HUANG (*politely*)   So it's Old Yang. Sit down, won't you? (*Indicates a seat.*)
> (YANG *dare not sit.*)

MU (*pouring tea*) Have some tea.

(YANG *remains silent*.)

HUANG Have you got everything ready for New Year, Old Yang?

YANG Well, sir, you know how it is. It's been snowing more than ten days, and we have no firewood or rice at home. I've not lit the stove for several days.

MU Bah! See here, Old Yang, there's no need to complain about poverty. Landlord Huang knows all about you, doesn't he?

HUANG Yes, Old Yang, I know you're not well off. But this year is passing, and I have to trouble you for the rent. (*Opens the account book*.) You cultivate one acre of my land. Last year you were five pecks short, this summer another four and a half pecks, in autumn another five and a half pecks.

MU (*reckoning on the abacus*) Five times five . . . two fives makes ten. . . .

HUANG And remember the money you owe us. In my father's time your wife died, and you wanted a coffin, so you borrowed five dollars from us. The year before last you were sick and borrowed two and a half dollars. Last year another three dollars. At that time we agreed upon five per cent monthly interest. At compound interest it amounts to—

MU (*reckoning on the abacus*) The interest on the interest amounts to—five times five, twenty-five. Two fives is ten. . . . Altogether twenty-five dollars fifty cents. Plus one and a half piculs' rent.

HUANG Altogether twenty-five dollars and fifty cents, and one and a half piculs' rent. Right, Old Yang?

YANG Yes, sir. . . . That's right.

HUANG See, Old Yang, it's down here quite clearly in black and white, all correct and in order. This is New Year's Eve, Old Yang: the rent must be

paid.   If you've got it with you, so much the better:
you pay the money and the debt is cancelled.   If you
haven't got it with you, then go and find some way
of raising it.   Steward Mu will go with you.

MU   So it's up to you.   I'm ready to go with you.
Get going, Old Yang!

YANG (*pleadingly*)   Oh, Mr. Mu....Sir....Please let
me off this time!   I really have no money, I can't
pay the rent or the debt.   (*His voice falters.*)
Sir....Mr. Mu....

HUANG   Now, Old Yang, that's no way to act.   This
is New Year's Eve.   You're in difficulties, but I'm
even worse off.   You must clear the debt today.

YANG   Sir....

HUANG   Come, you must be reasonable.   Whatever
you say, that debt must be paid.

MU   You heard what Landlord Huang said, Old Yang.
He never goes back on his word.   You must find a
way, Old Yang.

YANG   What can I do, sir?   An old man like me, with
no relatives or rich friends—where can I get money?
(*Beseechingly.*)   Sir....

HUANG (*seeing his opportunity, signals to* MU)
Well....

MU (*to* YANG)   Well, listen, Old Yang, there is a way.
Landlord Huang has thought of a way out for you,
if you will take it....

YANG   Tell me what it is, Mr. Mu.

MU   You go back, and bring your daughter Hsi-erh
here as payment for the rent.

YANG (*horror-stricken*)   What!

MU   Go and fetch Hsi-erh here as payment for the
rent.

YANG (*kneeling beseechingly*)   Sir, you can't do that!
(*Sings*) :
    The sudden demand for my girl as rent—

Is like thunder out of a cloudless sky!
Hsi-erh is the darling of my heart,
I'd rather die than lose her!
I beg you, sir,
Take pity on us, please,
And let me off this once!
She's all I have,
This is more than I can bear!

HUANG (*stands up in disgust*) Well, I'm doing you a good turn, Old Yang. Bring Hsi-erh to our house to spend a few years in comfort, and won't she be better off than in your home, where she has to go cold and hungry and has such a hard time of it? Besides, we are not going to treat Hsi-erh badly here. And this way your debt will be cancelled too. Isn't that killing two birds with one stone? (*Laughs.*)

YANG No, sir, you can't do that....

MU Well, Old Yang, it seems to me you poor people try to take advantage of the kindness of the rich. Landlord Huang wants to help your family. Just think, Hsi-erh coming here will have the time of her life. She will live on the fat of the land, dress like a lady and only have to stretch out her hand for food or drink! That would be much better than in your house where she goes cold and hungry. In fact Landlord Huang is quite distressed by all you make Hsi-erh put up with. So you'd better agree.

YANG But, sir, Mr. Mu, this child Hsi-erh is the apple of my eye. Her mother died when she was three, and I brought her up as best I could. I'm an old man now and I have only this daughter. She's both daughter and son to me. I can't let her go...sir! (*Turning to* HUANG.)

HUANG (*adamant*) Bah!

(YANG *turns to* MU *who also ignores him.*)

HUANG (*after a while*) I'm not going to wait any longer, Old Yang! Make your choice. Give me your girl or pay the debt.

MU Old Yang, Landlord Huang is in a good humour now. Don't offend him, or it'll be the worse for you.

HUANG (*angrily*) That's enough! Make out a statement! Tell him to send the girl tomorrow! (*Starts angrily off.*)

YANG (*stepping forward to clutch at him*) Don't go, sir!

HUANG Get away! (*Pushing* YANG *aside, he hurries off.*)

MU All right, better agree, Old Yang. (*Goes to the table to write a statement.*)

YANG (*barring* MU'S *way wildly*) You... you mustn't do that! (*Sings*):
  What have I done wrong,
  That I should be forced to sell my child?
  I've had a hard time of it all my life,
  But I little thought it would come to this!

MU Get wise, Old Yang. Don't keep on being such a fool. You've got to agree to this today, whether you like it or not! (*Pushes* YANG *aside and takes up a pen to write the statement.*)

YANG (*seizing* MU'S *hand*) No! (*Sings*):
  Heaven just kills the grass with a single root,
  The flood just carries off the one-plank bridge.
  She's the only child I ever had,
  And I can't live without her!

MU (*furiously*) Don't be a fool! Presently if you make the master lose his temper, it'll be no joke!

YANG I... I... I'll go somewhere to plead my case! (*About to rush out.*)

MU (*banging the table*) Where are you going to plead your case? The county magistrate is our friend, this is the yamen door; where are you going to plead your case!

YANG (*aghast*) I...I....

MU It's no use, Old Yang! You're no match for him. I advise you to make out a statement and put your mark on it to settle the business. (*Writes.*)

YANG (*stopping him again*) You...you....

(*Enter* HUANG *impatiently.*)

HUANG (*in a towering rage*) Why are you still so stubborn, Old Yang! Let me tell you, it's going to be done today, whether you like it or not! (*To* MU.) Hurry up and make out a statement for him.

YANG (*at a loss*) Ah!

MU (*reading as he writes*) "Tenant Yang owes Landlord Huang one and a half piculs of grain and twenty-five dollars fifty cents. Since he is too poor to pay, he wants to sell his daughter Hsi-erh to the landlord to cancel the debt. Both parties agree and will not go back on their word. Since verbal agreements are inconclusive, this statement is drawn up as evidence.... Signed by the two parties, Landlord Huang and Tenant Yang, and the witness, Steward Mu...." Right, talk is empty but writing is binding. Come on, Old Yang! Put your mark on it!

YANG (*frenziedly*) You can't do this, sir!

HUANG What! All right, then tell Liu to tie him up and take him to the county court!

YANG (*panic-stricken*) What, send me to the county court! Oh, sir!

MU (*seizing* YANG'S *hand*) Put your mark on it! (*Presses his fingers down.*)

YANG (*startled to see the ink on his finger*) Oh! (*Falls to the ground.*)

"You can't do this, sir!"

MU   Aha, one finger-print has cleared the debt of all these years.... (*Hands the document to* HUANG.)
   (HUANG *makes a gesture to* MU.)

MU (*ascertains that* YANG *is still breathing*) He's all right.

HUANG   Old Yang, you'd better go back now, and bring Hsi-erh here tomorrow. (*To* MU.)   Give him that document.

MU (*helping* YANG *up*)   This one is yours, here.... (*Hands him the document.*)   Tomorrow send Hsi-erh here to give New Year's greetings to Landlord Huang's family.   Tell her to come here to spend a happy New Year.   Go on.   (*Pushes* YANG *out, then shuts the door.*)
   (YANG *collapses outside the gate in the snow-storm.*)

HUANG   Old Mu, you take a few men there early tomorrow.   We don't want the old fellow to go back and decide to ignore the debt and run away. In that case we'd lose both girl and money.

MU   Right.

HUANG   Another thing.   For heaven's sake don't let word get about: it wouldn't sound well on New Year's Day.   If those wretches spread the news, even though we've right on our side it would be hard to explain.   If anyone questions you, say my mother wants to see Hsi-erh and you're fetching her to give New Year's greetings to the old lady.

MU   Very good.   (*Exit.*)

HUANG   Ah!   The only way to get rich is at the expense of the poor.   Without breaking Old Yang, I couldn't get Hsi-erh!

YANG (*comes to himself outside the gate, and gets up*)   Heaven!   Murderous Heaven! (*Sings*):
   Heaven kills folk without batting an eye!
   The landlord's house is Hell!

I'm an old fool, an old fool,
Why did I put my mark on that paper just now?
I've gone and sold my only daughter,
Your dad's let you down, Hsi-erh!
You're happy, waiting at home for me for New
    Year,
But I'm in despair!
With this hand I've sold my only child,
How can I face you when I get home?
(He staggers off.)

(*CURTAIN*)

Scene III

Yang's *old friend, the tenant peasant* Chao, *enters with a basket containing a small piece of meat and a pot of wine. He is taking the path by the village.*

Chao (*sings*):
    In the gale the snow whirls high,
    Nine homes out of ten are dimly lit;
    Not that we don't celebrate New Year,
    But the poor have a different New Year from
        the rich.
    There's wine and meat in the landlord's house,
    While we tenants have neither rice nor flour!
    (*He hears sounds of merriment from* Landlord Huang's *house in the distance.*) Bah! At New Year the rich could die of laughing, while the poor could die of despair! Old Yang's been away a week to escape paying his debt, but he ought to be back now. I've bought four ounces of wine to drink

with him. Getting his troubles off his chest is the poor man's way of spending New Year. (*Sings*):

> *Just as officials are all in league,*
> *The poor stick together too.*
> *I'm going to spend New Year's Eve with Old Yang,*
> *To share four ounces of cheap wine with a friend.* (*Exit.*)

(*Enter* YANG.)

YANG (*sings*):

> *I feel as befuddled as if I were drunk,*
> *In such a snowstorm where can I go?*
> *The deed in my pocket is like a knife*
> *That's going to kill my own flesh and blood.*

Where are you, Hsi-erh? You don't know what your dad.... (*Falls.*)

CHAO (*enters and sees a prostrate figure. When he goes to help him up he recognizes* YANG) So it's you, Old Yang?

YANG Who's that?

CHAO It's Old Chao.

YANG Oh, Old Chao, friend....

CHAO (*raising him*) What happened to you, Old Yang?

YANG Ah! (*For an instant he appears to be in a frenzy, but then fights down his feelings.*) Nothing .... No, nothing. Just now I went to the rich man's house....

CHAO Oh, so you were badly treated up there. It's snowing faster, let's go back now and talk it over. We'll have a good talk. (*Helps* YANG *along.*)

YANG Talk.... Talk.... Talk it over.... Have a good talk.

CHAO Here, how is it the door is closed? (*Opens the door and helps* YANG *in.*) Why is there no light? (*Gropes for the matches to light the lamp.*) Where are you, Hsi-erh?

YANG (*hearing* HSI-ERH'S *name*) Ah, Hsi-erh, Hsi-erh!

CHAO What is it, Old Yang?

YANG (*controlling himself*) Nothing, Hsi-erh has gone with Aunty Wang to make dumplings.

CHAO So this New Year's Eve you have dumplings to eat? Your daughter must be happy. Old Yang, look, I've got a pound of pork for you, for you two to eat tomorrow. And I've brought four ounces of wine. Tonight the two of us can drink a few cups. (*Heats the wine.*)

YANG Right, drink. Drink a few cups.... Drink a few cups. (*Sits by the stove. They drink.*)

CHAO What happened, Old Yang, in the landlord's house just now?

YANG That...nothing...Old Chao.

CHAO What is it? Tell me. I'm your friend.

YANG Ah, yes....

CHAO Go on, Old Yang! What's there to be afraid of?

YANG I....

CHAO You'd try the patience of a saint, the way you never take other people into your confidence, but keep all your troubles to yourself! But we two have always talked frankly, and tonight you mustn't brood. Come on, Old Yang, out with it!

YANG Very well, I'll tell you. I came home today, hoping to have escaped paying the debt. Then Steward Mu called me to the landlord's house.

CHAO Yes.

YANG Landlord Huang opened the account book and Mu reckoned on the abacus, and insisted on my clearing the debt. I couldn't pay it, so he....

CHAO So what?

YANG He wanted Hsi-erh as payment.

CHAO Did you agree?

YANG I.... No.

CHAO (*excitedly*) Good for you, Old Yang! You did right. To let Hsi-erh go to his house in payment for the debt would be like throwing your child to the wolves. As the proverb says, "Buddha needs incense, and a man needs self-respect." That's something we must fight for. You've shown the right spirit, Old Yang. (*Raises his cup.*) Come on, Old Yang, drink up.

YANG (*in agony of mind*) Old Chao...Old Chao, you know tomorrow—no, next year—next year the landlord will still want Hsi-erh to go.

CHAO Next year? Well, Old Yang, I'm considering that. Next year I'm not going to stay here. I'm going north.

YANG Where? Going north? Ah, even a poor home is hard to give up. If we leave, we'll starve.

CHAO Not necessarily. Here we cultivate these small plots of poor land, and can't live anyway, what with the rent. This year I worked fifty days for the landlord, but even so I didn't clear all the rent for the melon field; yesterday he was pressing me again. Bah! Why should an old man like me, all alone and without children, end my days on these small fields? I think we'd better take Hsi-erh to the north, until she's grown up. At our age, we can't expect to live long, and our death doesn't matter; but we mustn't ruin the child's life.

YANG (*sadly, weighing his words*) Our death doesn't matter, but we mustn't ruin the child's life.

CHAO Think it over, Old Yang! I consider next year, as soon as spring comes, we should take our things and go. (*Raises his cup again.*) Drink up!

YANG Ah!

(*Enter* AUNTY WANG, HSI-ERH *and* WANG TA-CHUN, *carrying the dumplings.*)

WANG Has Uncle Yang really come back, Ta-chun?

TA-CHUN I saw him coming out of the landlord's house. (*To* HSI-ERH.) Hsi-erh, the path is slippery, let me take that.

HSI-ERH I can carry it, Ta-chun.

(YANG, *hearing voices outside, hastily wipes his eyes and pretends all is well.*)

HSI-ERH (*approaching, sees a light through the door*) Aunty, I think Dad is really back. (*They enter.*)

HSI-ERH (*joyfully*) Dad, you're back!

TA-CHUN Uncle, you're back!

WANG Uncle Chao, you're here too....

CHAO We two have been chatting quite a time.

TA-CHUN Uncle, what happened in the landlord's house?

YANG I went, and couldn't pay the rent or settle the debt, so he....

ALL What did he do?

YANG Nothing...I...went down on my knees to him, that's all, and then came back.

TA-CHUN Really, Uncle?

HSI-ERH Really, Dad? That was all?

YANG Certainly, child. Have I ever deceived you?

CHAO That's right.

WANG (*wiping her eyes*) Thank heaven! All's well then, and we can enjoy New Year. Uncle Chao, we have a few pounds of flour not taken by the landlord, and we made some dumplings. You and Uncle Yang come and eat.

CHAO Right.

YANG Yes.

WANG   Ta-chun, empty out the garlic from that bowl, and give it to Uncle Yang. Hsi-erh, you take this one to Uncle Chao.

TA-CHUN   (*handing the bowl to* YANG) Try our dumplings, Uncle.

  (YANG *takes the bowl in silence.*)
  (*They eat.*)

HSI-ERH   (*sings*):
  Dad's come home after hiding from the duns!

TA-CHUN and WANG:
  We're eating dumplings for New Year!

ALL:
  Old and young we're sitting around,
  Enjoying a very happy New Year!
  Enjoying a happy New Year!

WANG:
  The snow's been falling for a week or more,

ALL:
  But we're all safely here together!

WANG:
  Hoping by the time our young folk grow up,

ALL:
  We can all pass some years in peace!
  Yes, pass some years in peace!

HSI-ERH   Dad, you aren't eating!

YANG   Yes, I am.

CHAO   (*reminiscently*) Ta-chun and Hsi-erh, today we're celebrating New Year and eating dumplings, so let me tell you a story about dumplings. It was 1930, the thirteenth day of the fifth moon, the day when the War God sharpened his sword. There was a fine rain falling. That day troops appeared from the southern mountains. They were called the Red Army.

WANG   So you're harping back to that, Uncle. Better eat now.

HSI-ERH   Let Uncle Chao talk, Aunty! I like to hear.

CHAO   Yes, they had red all over them, their red sashes bound crosswise from shoulder to waist; and they were all ruddy-faced, hefty fellows, so they were called the Red Army. They went south of the city to the Chao Village. I was there then, when the Red Army came and killed that devil, Landlord Chao. Then they distributed the grain and land among the poor, so on the thirteenth of the fifth moon all poor folk had basketfuls of white flour, and we all ate dumplings. In every house I went to then they offered me dumplings to eat.... (*Chuckles.*)

TA-CHUN   Where did that Red Army go to then?

CHAO   They went to the city, but they hadn't held it long when some Green Army arrived; then the Red Army went to the Great North Mountain, and never came down again. And after the Red Army left, the poor had a bad time of it once more.

TA-CHUN   Tell us, Uncle, will the Red Army be coming back?

CHAO   I think so.

HSI-ERH   When will they come?

CHAO   In good time, a day will come when the War God sharpens his sword again and the Red Army comes back. (*Chuckles.*)

WANG   Don't keep on talking but eat now. (*To* YANG.) Uncle, eat. There's plenty more.

HSI-ERH   Dad, have some more.

YANG (*holding the bowl, unable to eat, after a painful pause*)   Ah, Hsi-erh, isn't Aunty good?

HSI-ERH   Yes, she is!

YANG   Aunty, isn't Hsi-erh good?

WANG She's a good child.

YANG Hsi-erh, tell me, is your dad good?

HSI-ERH What a question! Of course you are, Dad!

YANG No, no.... Dad's no good.

WANG What's got into you, Uncle Yang? Why are you talking like this?

CHAO We've been drinking, and he may have had a drop too much.... (*Chuckles*.) It goes without saying you two are both good, Hsi-erh and Ta-chun. It won't be long now! (*Laughs*.)

(HSI-ERH *turns away shyly*.)

WANG Stop talking and eat!

YANG Yes, eat....

(*They all eat*.)

HSI-ERH (*sings*):
Dad's come home after hiding from the duns!

TA-CHUN and WANG:
We're eating dumplings for New Year!

ALL:
Old and young we're sitting around,
Enjoying a very happy New Year!
Enjoying a happy New Year!

WANG:
The snow's been falling for a week or more,

ALL:
But we're all here safely together!

WANG:
Hoping by the time our young folk grow up,

ALL:
We can all pass some years in peace!
Yes, pass some years in peace!

(*In a state of mental agony*, YANG *cannot keep still, so he withdraws to a corner, where he clutches the document in his pocket with trembling hands*.)

WANG What are you doing, Uncle Yang? Come and eat.

YANG (*startled*) I'm looking, looking.... Ah, it's empty, my pocket. Not a single coin. I can't even give the two youngsters money for New Year.

WANG   Come on.   To have dumplings is good enough. Come and eat, Uncle.

YANG   I...I'll eat later.

WANG   Uncle Chao, have some more.

CHAO   I've had enough.

WANG (*to* TA-CHUN *and* HSI-ERH)   How about you two?

TA-CHUN and HSI-ERH   We've had enough.

WANG   Then let's clear away.   (*They clear the table.*) Uncle Yang has been on his feet all day and is tired, he should rest now.

YANG (*mechanically*)   Rest now.

WANG   We would go on chatting forever, but we can talk again tomorrow.   Tomorrow Ta-chun will come to give you New Year greetings.

CHAO   I'll be going too.   Hsi-erh, take good care of your dad.   Old Yang, tomorrow I'll come and wish you a happy New Year.   I'm off now.

YANG   Good night, Old Chao.

   (*Exit* CHAO.)

TA-CHUN   We're going too, Uncle.

YANG   See your mother back carefully, Ta-chun.

HSI-ERH   Are you going, Aunty!

WANG   Good night. (*She and* TA-CHUN *go out.*)
   (HSI-ERH *starts to close the door.*)

TA-CHUN (*at the door*)   Hsi-erh, Uncle is tired!   Get him to rest early.

HSI-ERH   Yes. (*Closes the door.* WANG *and* TA-CHUN *go out.*)

YANG   You'd better go to bed, Hsi-erh.

HSI-ERH   So had you, Dad.

YANG   Your dad...your dad will see the New Year in.

HSI-ERH   I'll stay up too.

YANG   Then put on some more firewood.

   (HSI-ERH *adds wood to the stove and sits by the fire.*)

YANG (*coughing*)   Hsi-erh, your dad is old and good for nothing.

HSI-ERH   Whatever do you mean, Dad! Come and warm yourself!

   (*They sit by the stove. The silence is oppressive, while snow falls outside. Time passes.*)

YANG   Are you asleep, Hsi-erh?

HSI-ERH   No, Dad . . . .

YANG   I'll trim the lamp. (*He trims the lamp.*) (*Presently the lamp on the stove burns low, and* HSI-ERH *falls asleep.*) The wick is burnt out, and the oil is used up. (*The lamp goes out.*) The light is out too...Hsi-erh! (HSI-ERH *is sound asleep.*)

YANG   Asleep? Hsi-erh! (*Sings*) :

   Hsi-erh, my child, you're sleeping,
   Dad calls you, but you don't hear.
   You can't imagine, as you dream,
   The unforgivable thing I've done.

   Hsi-erh, Dad has wronged you! Aunty Wang, I've wronged you! Old Chao, I've wronged you! I made a statement and put my mark on it. . . . When Hsi-erh's mother died, she said, "Bring Hsi-erh up as best you can." And I brought her up. Hsi-erh has had a hard time of it with me for seventeen years. Today...I've wronged Hsi-erh's mother, I've sold our child. . . . Tomorrow the landlord will take her away. Neither the living nor the dead, neither human beings nor ghosts can ever forgive me! I'm an old fool, a criminal! But I can't let you go! I'll have it out with them! (*He runs wildly out, to be buffeted by the wind and snow.*) Ah, magistrates, landlords!... Lackeys. . . . Bailiffs!... Where can

I go? Where can I turn? (*He clutches the document.*) Ah! (*Sings*):

Magistrates, rich men—you tigers and wolves!
Because I owed rent and was in debt,
You forced me to write a deed,
Selling my child....
The north wind's blowing, snow's falling thick
*   and fast!*
Where can I go? Where can I fly?
What way out is there for me?

(*He pauses, bewildered.*) Ah, I still have some lye for making beancurd—I'll drink that! (*He drinks it.*) Now I'll drink some cold water.... (*He takes off his padded jacket to cover* HSI-ERH, *then rushes outside, falls on the snow and dies.*)

(*Crackers sound in the village, signalling the arrival of the New Year.*)

(*CURTAIN*)

SCENE IV

Crackers sound and TA-CHUN *comes in gaily.*

TA-CHUN   Uncle Yang! Uncle Yang! I've come to wish you a happy New Year! (*He suddenly stumbles on the corpse.*) Oh! (*Clearing the snow from the face of the dead man he recognizes* YANG.) Oh! Uncle Yang! You! What's happened? (*He hurries to the door and knocks.*) Hsi-erh, Hsi-erh! Open the door, quick! (*Hastily turning towards the backstage.*) Mother! Mother! Come quick! Come quick!

HSI-ERH (*wakened from her sleep*) Dad! Dad! (*She looks for her father.*)

TA-CHUN Hsi-erh! (*Pushing open the door.*) Hsi-erh! Look! Your dad—

HSI-ERH Has something happened to Dad? (*Runs out, and seeing her father's body, falls on it and cries.*) Dad! Dad!

TA-CHUN What happened, Hsi-erh?

HSI-ERH (*cries. Then sings*):
> Yesterday evening when Dad came back,
> He was worried but wouldn't tell me why.
> This morning he's lying in the snow!
> Why, Dad, why?

TA-CHUN (*helplessly turning towards the backstage*) Mother, come quick!

(*Enter* AUNTY WANG.)

WANG What is it, Ta-chun?

TA-CHUN Mum, look at Uncle Yang! He—(*Pointing to the corpse.*)

WANG What's happened to Uncle Yang? (*She kneels beside the corpse and touches it, hoping the dead man will wake up.*) Ta-chun, go and call Uncle Chao and the others at once.

(*Exit* TA-CHUN.)

WANG (*finding the body stiff and lifeless, wails*) Uncle Yang! Uncle Yang!

HSI-ERH Daddy! (*Cries.*)

(*Enter* TA-CHUN *with* UNCLE CHAO, LI *and* TA-SO.)

CHAO What's happened?

TA-SO What happened, Ta-chun?

LI It's Old Yang.

WANG (*crying as she tells the story*) Friends, last night when he came back he was all right. Who could imagine this morning he would—(*Unable to proceed.*)

CHAO (*stoops and examines* YANG) He's drunk lye.

HSI-ERH Daddy!

CHAO (*noticing the dead man's clenched fist*) Ah! (*He starts forcing open the fingers.* TA-CHUN *and* TA-SO *help him, and they take the deed of sale.*)

LI (*reading the deed*) Tenant Yang owes Landlord Huang rent.... Since he is too poor to pay, he wants to sell his daughter Hsi-erh to.... (*Unable to finish he lets the deed fall to the ground. They are all horror-stricken.*)

WANG Merciful heavens! This....

HSI-ERH (*shrieks*) Oh, Dad! (*Sings*):
Suddenly hearing that I've been sold,
I feel as if fire were burning me!
Could it be Dad didn't love me?
Or thought me a bad daughter, could it be?

CHAO (*addressing the corpse indignantly*) Old Yang, last night you only told me half! You shouldn't have died! Because you wouldn't leave your little patch of land, you let them hound you to death!

TA-SO (*loudly*) Last night they took away my donkey! Today for this paltry rent they drove Uncle Yang to suicide! They won't let the poor live! It's too much! (*Too angry to speak he turns to rush out.*)

TA-CHUN (*unable to suppress his anger*) They killed Uncle Yang, and they make Hsi-erh.... I'm going to have it out with them! (*He rushes after* TA-SO.)

    (CHAO *and* LI *pull* TA-SO *back, while* AUNTY WANG *restrains* TA-CHUN.)

WANG Ta-chun! Ta-chun!

LI It's no good, Ta-so, Ta-chun! It's there in black and white! Uncle Yang put his mark on it.

TA-CHUN His mark? They forced him, didn't they? I'll send in an appeal!

TA-SO Right!

LI (*sighs*) To whom can you appeal? The district
head? The magistrate? Aren't they hand in glove
with the rich? I think we'd better accept it, if we
can.

TA-SO Accept it? I can't!

TA-CHUN How are we poor folk to live! (*Stamps his
foot and strikes his head in despair.*)

CHAO Ta-chun, Ta-so, blustering is no use. Time's
getting on, and the landlord will soon be here to
fetch the girl; we'd better hurry to prepare the dead
for burial, so that Hsi-erh can at least attend her
father's funeral. We all know what goes on
nowadays, but they've got the whip hand. Where
can we turn to look for justice?... (*To* HSI-ERH.)
This has happened today because we old people are
no good: we've done you a great wrong, child! Ta-
chun, Ta-so, we'd better first bury the dead! Aunty
Wang, get ready quickly, and put Hsi-erh in mourning!

(*They bow their heads in silence, wiping their
eyes in sorrow and anger.*)

(*Enter* STEWARD MU *with thugs.*)

MU A happy New Year, friends! I wish you good
luck and prosperity!

(*They are all taken aback.*)

MU (*seeing the dead man in their midst, realizes what
has happened, but feigns astonishment*) Ah! Who's
that?

LI It's Old Yang.

MU What, Old Yang!... Why, last night he was all
right, how could he...? Well, well.... (*Feigning
sympathy.*) Who could have thought it? Such an
honest fellow.... (*Turns.*) Well then...let us all
help, and prepare his funeral.... Oh, Hsi-erh is
here. Let's do it this way: let Hsi-erh come with

me to beg the landlord for a coffin for her father. Come on, Hsi-erh. (*Tries to lead* HSI-ERH *off.*)

TA-CHUN (*unable to contain his anger, darts forward and shakes his fist at* MU, *who steps aside*) I know why you've come. You shan't take her!

TA-SO (*stepping forward too*) You dare!

THUGS (*stepping forward to cover* TA-CHUN *and* TA-SO *with their guns*) Hey, there! Don't move!

MU (*changing his tune*) All right, let's put our cards on the table. Old Yang has sold Hsi-erh to Landlord Huang! Here's the deed. (*Taking the deed from his pocket.*) Old Yang put his mark on it, so justice and reason are on our side.... Sorry, Wang Ta-chun, but Hsi-erh belongs to the landlord now.

TA-CHUN Steward Mu, you dog aping your master, bullying the poor!

MU So! You are cursing me? Very well, fellow, just wait and see!

CHAO Mr. Mu, this is too much. The child's father has just died, and you want to carry her off, on New Year's Day too.

MU Too much? (*Pointing to the deed.*) Here's our reason. Better mind your own business.

WANG Mr. Mu, let the child attend the funeral first....

MU Can't be done. Landlord Huang wants the girl taken back immediately. (*Sizing up the situation he adopts a more conciliatory tone.*) Well, actually I can't make any decisions; you must talk to Landlord Huang. Still, I think Hsi-erh will enjoy herself later on. (*He takes hold of* HSI-ERH *again.*) Come on, Hsi-erh.

TA-CHUN and TA-SO You!... (*They want to rush forward again, but are stopped by the guns of the thugs.*)

(AUNTY WANG *timidly steps in front of* TA-CHUN.)

CHAO (*signing to them to stop*) Ta-chun! Ta-so!

HSI-ERH (*shaking off* MU'S *hand, darts back to* CHAO *and* AUNTY WANG) Uncle! Aunty! (*Rushing to the dead man, she cries bitterly.*) Daddy! Daddy!...

MU (*pulling at* HSI-ERH *again*) Well, Hsi-erh, we're all mortal. It's no use crying, better come with me. (*Pulls hard.*)

HSI-ERH (*frightened, screams and struggles*) Uncle! Aunty!

WANG Steward Mu, do let the child put on mourning for her father.

MU All right, put on mourning.

(AUNTY WANG *goes inside and fetches out a piece of white cloth which she ties round* HSI-ERH'S *head.*)

CHAO (*holding* HSI-ERH, *speaks to the dead man*) Old Yang, Hsi-erh can't attend your funeral today. This is all the fault of us old folk, we've done her a wrong. (*To* HSI-ERH.) Come, Hsi-erh, kowtow to your father.

HSI-ERH Uncle! Aunty! (*Kneels and kowtows.*)

(MU *drags* HSI-ERH *off crying and screaming, followed by* AUNTY WANG. TA-CHUN *and* TA-SO *want to pursue them, but are stopped by* CHAO.)

CHAO Ta-chun, Ta-so.... They have the whip hand, what can we do? Let us remember how many people the Huang family has killed. Their day of reckoning will come! A day will come when power changes hands.... (*They sob.*) Don't cry, but come and bury the dead!

(*They carry* YANG *off.*)

(*CURTAIN*)

ACT II

SCENE I

TIME   *As in the last scene.*
The Buddhist shrine of LANDLORD HUANG'S *mother.*
  Big, bright candles are lit, and incense smoke
  wreathes the air.
MRS. HUANG *comes in bearing incense sticks in her*
  hand.

MRS. HUANG   Yesterday my son told me our tenant
  Yang was sending his daughter here as payment
  for the rent.   Why hasn't she come to see me yet?
  (*Sings*) :
      At New Year our family gains in wealth and we
          old folk in longevity,
      Thanks to the virtues of our ancestors and holy
          Buddha's protection.
      I carry incense to the shrine where bright candles
          are lit on the altar,
      And bow three times in all sincerity.
      One stick of incense I offer Ju-lai of the Western
          Heaven—
      May we grow wealthy, and our rents increase!
      The second stick I offer Kuan-yin of the Southern
          Seas—
      Grant peace in the four seasons, and may all our
          house grow rich!

The third stick I offer Chang Hsien, giver of children—
Protect us, and may we increase and multiply!
(She closes the door and sits down.)

Now money is depreciating: one maidservant costs so many years' rent! Last year was better, when we bought that girl Hung-lu for only eight dollars; while that girl bought by the northern household only cost five dollars and fifty cents. But this year everything is expensive!

(MU comes on with HSI-ERH.)

MU   Come along, Hsi-erh. *(Sings)*:
What a queer girl you are!
Why act so strangely here?
Just now, when we saw the landlord,
You wouldn't look up or say a word,
And when he gave you a flower,
You wouldn't wear it!
Now that we're going to see the old lady,
You'll have to be on your best behaviour!
Look happy now!

(HSI-ERH gives a frightened sob.)

MU   Don't cry! If you make the old lady angry, even with her fingers she can scratch holes in your face. *(They enter the room.)* Ah, Mrs. Huang, the Yang family girl, Hsi-erh, has come to give you her New Year greetings.

MRS. HUANG   Oh, it's Old Mu. Come in. *(Enter MU and HSI-ERH.)*

MU *(to HSI-ERH)*   Kowtow to the mistress! *(Pushes her down on her knees.)*

MRS. HUANG   All right, get up.

MU *(raising HSI-ERH)*   Get up, and let the mistress look at you.

MRS. HUANG   H'm, a good-looking child. Come over here.

MU (*to* HSI-ERH) Go on. (*He drags her again.*)

MRS. HUANG The child looks intelligent. What's her name?

(HSI-ERH *remains silent.*)

MU Answer the mistress. You're called...called Hsi-erh.

MRS. HUANG Hsi-erh? Well, that's an auspicious name.[1] It needn't be altered much to match Hung-fu and Hung-lu; we'll just add the word Hung in front. Let her be called Hung-hsi.

MU (*to* HSI-ERH) Thank the mistress for your new name. From now on you won't be called Hsi-erh but Hung-hsi.

MRS. HUANG How old is the child?

(HSI-ERH *remains silent.*)

MU Seventeen.

MRS. HUANG Ah, seventeen. Good girl, better than Hung-fu. Hung-fu is a regular scarecrow, she looks like nothing on earth! This girl is good. Old Mu, presently you tell my son I shall keep her with me.

MU Oh! That's too good for her.

MRS. HUANG Well, her family is poor. Think of the hardships her father made her suffer—nothing to eat, no clothes to wear. Now that you've come to our house, Hung-hsi, you'll live in comfort. Are you glad?

(HSI-ERH *remains silent.*)

MU Speak up.... You are glad, you are glad! You are a lucky girl!

MRS. HUANG See, the girl is dressed like a beggar! Old Mu, tell my maid Chang to change her clothes and bring her cakes to eat.

---

[1] "Hsi" means "joy."

MU (*calling*) Ta-sheng! (*There is a response off-stage.*) The mistress orders Chang to change Hung-hsi's clothes and bring cakes for Hung-hsi!

    (*Voice offstage:* "Yes, mistress! Visitors have come from the north village to pay their respects to you and Landlord Huang.")

MRS. HUANG All right. (*Stands up. To* HSI-ERH.) Hung-hsi, soon Chang will come to change your clothes and look after you. (*Starting out.*) Ah, who-ever does good deeds in his life will become a Buddha and go to the Western Paradise. (MRS. HUANG *and* MU *leave.*)

    (*Voices off:* "We've come to pay our respects to Mrs. Huang!" "We've come to wish Landlord Huang a happy New Year!")

HSI-ERH Oh dear! (*Sings*):

Oh, Dad!
I hear so many voices here,
I'm all of a tremble!
So many bolts, so many doors!
I call my dad, but he doesn't answer.
Who'll wear mourning for my dad?
Who'll cry at his funeral?

    (*Enter* TA-SHENG *holding a plate, and* CHANG *with clothes.*)

TA-SHENG So this is Hung-hsi. Here, come and eat your cake.

CHANG You must be hungry, have something to eat.

TA-SHENG Hurry. I have to go and look after the guests.

    (*Out of nervousness* HSI-ERH *drops the plate and breaks it.*)

TA-SHENG What a bad girl you are, breaking a plate on New Year's Day! I'm going to tell the old lady.

CHANG Don't, Ta-sheng! (*Picks up the broken pieces.*) The old lady's in a good temper today;

don't make her angry. The girl's just come, she doesn't know how to behave. Let her off this time.

TA-SHENG Huh, little wretch! We'll wait and see how she behaves in future. (*Exit.*)

CHANG Hung-hsi, come with me to change your clothes. (*Taking her arm.*) Child, this is not your own home, not like with your own parents; you'll have to fit in with these people's ways.... Come, don't be afraid. I'm Aunty Chang, I'm a servant too. We shall be together a long time; if there's anything you can't do, I'll help you. If you have any trouble, let me know.... Come now, come and change your clothes. (*Exeunt.*)

(*CURTAIN*)

SCENE II

TIME *One month later.*

PLACE *At the gate of* AUNTY WANG'S *house.*

Enter TA-CHUN.

TA-CHUN (*sings*):

Uncle Yang's been dead for a month, and Hsi-erh
In the landlord's house is treated like dirt;
My mother's in tears the whole of the time,
And it's harder than ever to make ends meet.
How can I ever get even with them?
My whole heart seems to burn with hate!
When I went just now to look for Hsi-erh,
Huang's thugs wouldn't let me in at the gate!

(*Stamps.*) Today I wanted to go and see Hsi-erh in my spare time, but that gateman saw me.... It was Ta-so who suggested that some day, when I had time, I should fetch Hsi-erh out; but although I've been there several times, I haven't been able to see her. Yesterday Landlord Huang pressed me to pay my debt, saying if I didn't pay they'd evict me, and drive me away. This evening Steward Mu's coming again. Bah! (*He pushes open the door and goes in.*) Mother! (*No one answers.*) She must have gone over to see Uncle Chao. When she gets back there'll be more sighing and sobbing. (*Enter* TA-SO.)

TA-SO   Ta-chun!

TA-CHUN   Who is it?

TA-SO   Me! (*Coming forward.*) My! That bastard Mu has got his knife into us! Just now when I was out, he went to my home and took away five pints of kaoliang seeds, driving my mother nearly frantic. Some day that bastard's going to get what's coming to him....

TA-CHUN   I've just come back from the Huang house. It was no good, I still couldn't see Hsi-erh.... (*Pauses.*) Presently Steward Mu is going to throw me out....

TA-SO   What, is he coming soon? (*Looking at the sky.*) It's getting dark.... (*Looking at the door.*) Is your mother home?

TA-CHUN   No.

TA-SO   Ta-chun, I think we ought to have a fling at him tonight!

TA-CHUN   What do you mean, Ta-so?

TA-SO   When the bastard comes, we'll (*makes a gesture and whispers*)....

TA-CHUN   (*worked up*) Yes... but... if it leaked out, my mother and Hsi-erh....

TA-SO   Don't be afraid. It's dark, and when we're through with the rogue we'll drag him to the North Mountain gully to feed the wolves! (*He whispers again.*)

TA-CHUN All right, we'll be ready for him this evening! (*The watch sounds.* TA-CHUN *and* TA-SO
take cover, and TA-CHUN *fetches a rope from the
house.*)

(*Enter* MU, *weaving tipsily.*)

MU (*sings*) :
Kings and queens, kings and queens,
And all the aces too!
I don't care for kings or queens,
All I want, my knave, is you!
(*Laughing he reaches the gate.*) Ta-chun! Ta-
chun! Why haven't you gone yet, you rascal? Clear
out of the house and be off with you!

(TA-CHUN *remains angrily silent.*)

MU You want to spend all your life here, don't you,
you rogue! You won't give up! Today you were
hanging about the Huangs' gate again! Do you
still want another man's girl? True, Hsi-erh was
promised to you before, but she belongs to our Landlord Huang now.... Ah, that wench! Let me tell
you, Landlord Huang knows you won't keep quiet,
you rogue, so he says we've got to get rid of you.
You clear out of this house now, and look sharp
about it! (*He advances as he speaks.* TA-CHUN
does not answer, and as MU *approaches he falls
back.*) Where are you going, fellow? Why don't
you say something?... Where are you going?
(*Pressing* TA-CHUN.)

(TA-SO *suddenly seizes* MU *from behind and
throws him to the ground.*)

MU Who's that?

TA-SO Don't you dare shout! (*To* TA-CHUN.) Stop his
mouth, Ta-chun. (MU *struggles.*)

TA-SO You're going to dun for debts in hell! (*As they
beat* MU, *two of* LANDLORD HUANG'S *thugs enter.*)

THUGS What's up?

(TA-CHUN *and* TA-SO, *seeing them, start to make off but are seized. However* TA-CHUN *breaks loose and escapes.*)

THUGS (*helping* MU *up*)   Well, Mr. Mu, you've had a fright!

MU (*panting*)   Lao San, Lao San—go after him! Go after Wang Ta-chun! (*Pointing to* TA-SO.) Well, so it was you, Ta-so, my fine fellow!.... Old Liu, take him back for questioning.

(TA-SO *is pushed off by the thugs, kicking and struggling.* MU *also leaves.*)

(*The inner curtain falls.*)

(TA-CHUN *hurries in, and hammers at the door.*)

TA-CHUN   Uncle Chao!   Uncle Chao!

(CHAO *enters.*)

TA-CHUN   Uncle Chao, where's my mother?

CHAO   She's gone home, Ta-chun. Why have you got the wind up like this?

TA-CHUN   Uncle, something's happened! Ta-so and I beat up Steward Mu, but we were found out, and Ta-so was caught. Now they're after me!

CHAO   You young fellows! Just rashness is no use. I knew you were smouldering with rage, but our time hasn't come yet, Ta-chun. You can't stay here now; you'd better make off quickly.

TA-CHUN   Uncle....

CHAO   Go northwest, quickly!

TA-CHUN   Uncle...my mother and Hsi-erh....

CHAO   I'll look after them. Go now. When times change, you can come back and see your mother and me.

(TA-CHUN *runs off, and* CHAO *goes out.*)

(*CURTAIN*)

SCENE III

The HUANG *house.*
Enter LANDLORD HUANG *holding a lantern.*

HUANG (*sings*):
    Fate's been kind to me, I'm rich and respected,
    My barns are stuffed with grain and my chests
        with gold.
    The poor, of course, must go cold and hungry,
    Because that's their destiny, fixed by Fate!
    If cattle won't budge, I whip them;
    If pigs won't die, I slaughter them;
    And if the poor set themselves against me,
    They'll find out to their cost what fools they've
        been!
A few days ago Ta-so and Ta-chun refused to pay their rent, and beat up Steward Mu. Tch! It's really preposterous! They should remember who I am.... Even rats think twice before coming out of their holes. Do they think they can get anywhere by making an enemy of me? Ta-so I have sent to the district jail. Ta-chun ran away, but let him go! I don't think he dares to come back even if he wants to. As for Hsi-erh.... (*Chuckles.*) The only trouble is she's kept by my mother, so I've not been able to get hold of her yet, which is beginning to make me impatient.... Today I went to the north village to feast with some friends, and I'm feeling rather restless. Now that it's dark I'll go and have another try at it—try, try and try again!... (*Laughs.*)
   (*The second watch sounds, showing that it is after ten.*)
   (*Sings*):
Hearing the second watch,
I tiptoe to my mother's room.

> *I've hit on a fine plan*
> *To get my way tonight.*
> (*Exit.*)
>
> (*The back curtain rises, disclosing* MRS. HUANG'S *bedroom.*)
>
> (*Enter* HSI-ERH, *carrying broth.*)

HSI-ERH (*sings*) :
> *The few months I've been here,*
> *My life has been so bitter—*
> *First I am cursed, then beaten,*
> *They treat me all the time like dirt.*
> *But I have to swallow my tears,*
> *My only friend is Aunty Chang.*

> (*She approaches the left side of the bed, and calls timidly:* "Mistress!" *Then approaches the right side of the bed and calls again,* "Mistress! Mistress!")

Ah! (*Sings*) :
> *Rich people are hard to please,*
> *I haven't a minute to myself;*
> *And if I'm careless and annoy her,*
> *I'm afraid she may do me in!*

> (*Voice from within the bed curtains:* "Hung-hsi, is the lotus-seed broth ready?")

HSI-ERH   Coming, mistress! (*A hand comes out from the curtain to take the bowl.*)

> (*Voice from the bed:* "So hot! Do you want to scald me? You damn slave! Cool it!" *She passes the bowl back.*)

HSI-ERH (*holding the bowl, sings*) :
> *It's either too hot or too cold,*
> *She's never satisfied.*
> *I'm so tired and sleepy,*
> *But it's more than my life's worth to sleep!*

> (*Voice from the bed:* "Give me the broth!")

HSI-ERH   Coming, mistress! (*A hand from the bed takes the bowl.*)

(*Voice from the bed:* "What, so bitter? You can't have taken out the roots properly. You make me furious, damn you! Kneel down!")

HSI-ERH (*frightened*) I...I.... (*Kneels.*)

(*Voice from the bed:* "You bitch, who can drink such bitter broth? Open your mouth!" *Reaching out with an opium pin she slashes at* HSI-ERH'S *mouth.*)

HSI-ERH Oh! (*Cries.*)

(HUANG *steals on, and listens at the door.*)

(*Voice from the bed:* "Don't cry! You really are infuriating!")

HSI-ERH I...I.... (*Cries.*)

(*Voice from the bed, angrily:* "Damn slave!" *She parts the bed curtain and emerges.*)

MRS. HUANG Damn slave! (*Beats her again and again with a feather duster.*)

HUANG (*coming in quickly to stop her*) Mother, Mother, don't be angry! Mother! (*Helps her to the bed.*)

MRS. HUANG What brings you here?... (*To* HSI-ERH.) Get up. (HSI-ERH *gets up.*)

HUANG Don't be angry, Mother. You're not feeling well these days, and Hung-hsi has offended you....

MRS. HUANG What brings you here so late?

HUANG I came to see you, and...I would like Hung-hsi to sew something for me.

MRS. HUANG I need Hung-hsi to make my broth.

HUANG Oh....

MRS. HUANG My, how you reek of wine! Better go to bed at once!

HUANG Yes, Mother....Yes...er...Mother, you rest and have some opium. Don't be angry. (HUANG *prepares the opium pipe for his mother, who smokes; then he puts down the bed curtains.*)

HUANG Come, Hung-hsi, come.

HSI-ERH (*in alarm*) Young master, you....

MRS. HUANG   Son, what are you doing?   Haven't you gone yet?

HUANG   Mother, I was saying that Hung-hsi is quite clever, isn't she (*taking* HSI-ERH'S *hand*), at looking after you!... (*Pinches her arm.*)
(HSI-ERH *gives a scream.*)

MRS. HUANG (*angrily getting out of bed again and sitting down*)   You wretched slave, have you gone crazy again?

HUANG   Er...er...Mother, I think tomorrow I'd better ask Dr. Chen from the town to examine you again.

MRS. HUANG   Humph!
(*Enter* CHANG, *and sets a teapot on the bed.*)

CHANG (*sizing up the situation*)   Has Hung-hsi offended you again, mistress? (*To* HUANG.) Why are you here, sir?   It's getting late, you should rest now.

HUANG (*to himself*)   Huh, this servant Chang....

CHANG   The old lady is not feeling well and it's getting late.... Better go to bed, sir.

MRS. HUANG   Go to bed, son.

CHANG (*nudging* HSI-ERH)   Sir, here's your lantern. (*Passing him the lantern.*)

MRS. HUANG   Go on back, son. Hung-hsi, prepare that broth for me.

HUANG   Well, Mother, you'd better sleep. (*To* CHANG.)   Tomorrow you wash those clothes of mine.

CHANG   Yes, sir.
(*Exit* HUANG.)

CHANG   Hsi-erh, come and heat the old lady's broth.
(HSI-ERH *moves to take the bowl, but* CHANG *signs to her to be seated, and heats the broth herself.*)
(HSI-ERH *remains silent, and they watch the broth.*)

CHANG (*softly letting down the curtains*) How did you offend the old lady, Hung-hsi?

HSI-ERH She said I hadn't taken the roots out of the lotus seeds, and they tasted bitter; but I had picked them clean....

CHANG (*indignantly*) Well! She feels bitter because she's had too much opium....

> (*Voice from the bed:* "Chang! What are you talking about?")

CHANG I was telling Hung-hsi not to cry, so as not to wake you....

> (*Voice from the bed:* "Oh....")
> (*Silence.*)

CHANG (*softly*) Hung-hsi, you couldn't have had enough to eat this evening. (*Taking a dumpling from her sleeve.*) Have this.

HSI-ERH (*biting eagerly into the dumpling, gives a cry because her mouth hurts*) Oh!

CHANG (*surprised*) What's the matter? (*Looks at the wound.*) Oh, so she's hurt you with the opium pin again.... (*Indignantly.*) Well! Presently I'll go to the kitchen and get some soup for you.

HSI-ERH (*in pain*) No... no need.

CHANG (*looking at* MRS. HUANG) Well, the old lady is asleep.... (*Sits by* HSI-ERH *and fans the fire.*) Ah, Hung-hsi, it's a hard, hard life. Only we two know it. It was because my family couldn't pay our rent either that I was sent to work here in payment for the rent. The things I've seen during these years! Every single maidservant like us has a wretched life of it. (*She sighs, then pauses.*) Hung-hsi, I'll tell you something, but you mustn't let it upset you....

HSI-ERH Yes, Aunty.

CHANG Ta-chun and Ta-so, because the landlord pressed them for rent, beat up Steward Mu. Ta-so

was caught and put in jail, and Ta-chun ran
away....

HSI-ERH   Oh! (*She starts crying from the shock.*)

CHANG (*comforting her*)   It happened nearly a month
ago; but I didn't tell you for fear it might upset
you....

HSI-ERH   Then...Aunty Wang?

CHANG   Don't worry, your Uncle Chao's looking after
her.... That's how it is, and it's no use crying over
spilt milk.   We're all in the same boat; although
life is so hard, we have to stick it out....

    (HSI-ERH *cries.*)

    (*The third watch sounds.*)

CHANG   That's the third watch now.... The old lady
is asleep, and the master should have gone to bed
too.   When the broth is ready, Hung-hsi, come back
to bed; don't run around.   I'll wait for you. (*Exit.*)

HSI-ERH (*goes on watching the broth, and sings*) :

    It's after midnight now,
    The more I think, the sadder I grow.
    Poor Dad was hounded to death,
    And Ta-chun forced to leave home.
    Why must we poor folk suffer so?
    Why are the rich so cruel?
    How can we go on living like this?
    Will these hard times never end?

    (*She dozes and the broth boils. Sh starts up to re-
move the pot from the fire, but lets it fall.   The pot
is broken and the broth spilled.* MRS. HUANG *snores.*)

HSI-ERH (*sings*) :

    I'm dizzy and I feel so frightened;
    I've broken the pot and spilt the broth!
    Now I've done such a dreadful thing,
    I'm afraid I shan't escape with my life!
    Where can I hide myself?
    Oh, Heaven, save me!

(*As she runs out, the back curtain falls.* HSI-ERH *re-enters from the side of the curtain, and sings*):
At dead of night it's so dark,
The road is black and everywhere there are dogs.
I can hear someone coming after me;
I can't escape this time!
(*Enter* HUANG *with a lantern to confront her.* HSI-ERH *halts in dismay.*)

HUANG (*overjoyed*)   Aha, what luck! What brought you here, Hung-hsi ?

HSI-ERH (*frightened*)   I...I.... (*Wants to leave.*)

HUANG (*seizing her*)   Ah! Hung-hsi, sew something on for me! I need it now. Come, come on over! (*Pushes open the door. The back curtain opens. He pushes* HSI-ERH *in and bolts the door behind him. This is* LANDLORD HUANG'S *study. A painting of a big tiger hangs there. The tiger is crouching, ready to spring.*)

HSI-ERH (*terrified*)   Oh! (*She turns to fly, but is pushed aside by* HUANG.)

HUANG (*seizing* HSI-ERH'S *hand*)   Come, Hung-hsi. (*His eyes gleam with lust, as he pushes* HSI-ERH.) Come on!

HSI-ERH   Oh! (*Struggling.*)   Aunty! Aunty! (*She starts running, but is pushed into the inner room.*)

HUANG   You! Ha! Still shouting! You won't escape now! Come on! (*Follows* HSI-ERH *inside.*)
(*The fifth watch is heard. Day gradually dawns.*)

(*CURTAIN*)

SCENE IV

CHANG *enters hurriedly.*

CHANG   Hung-hsi! Hung-hsi! (*Sings*):
> *Last night she was beaten and frightened,*
> *So I stayed with her till it was late.*
> *Only when all was quiet, at midnight,*
> *And she had calmed down, I came back.*
> *But this morning she's not to be found,*
> *Though I've looked for her everywhere.*
> *Hung-hsi! Hung-hsi!* (*Exit.*)

(*Enter* HSI-ERH *with dishevelled hair and crumpled clothes. Her face is tear-stained, and she walks with difficulty.*)

HSI-ERH (*comes to the door, but shrinks from opening it. Sings*):
> *Heaven!*
> *You could kill me with a knife or axe,*
> *But you shouldn't have shamed me!*
> *I little thought of this*
> *When I came to the Huang house....*
> *Mother bore me, Dad brought me up,*
> *Was it all for nothing?*
> *Now—how can I face people?*
> *How can I live on?*

Oh, Dad, Dad, I've let you down! Aunty Wang, Ta-chun, I can never face you again! (*Having decided to commit suicide, she finds a rope in a corner of the room, and picks it up.*)   Oh, Dad, Dad, I'm coming. (*Ties the rope to a rafter.*)

(CHANG *enters and sees her through a crack of the door.*)

CHANG   Hung-hsi, let me in!

HSI-ERH (*startled*)   Oh! (*The rope falls from her trembling hands.*)

CHANG   Hung-hsi! Open the door for me, quickly!

HSI-ERH (*opens the door, and runs to* CHANG *as she enters*)   Aunty! (*Cries.*)

CHANG   Hung-hsi!   You—

HSI-ERH   I...I....

CHANG   (*seeing the rope, understands*)   Hung-hsi, how could you think of such a thing?   You must never...never....

HSI-ERH   Aunty!   (*Cries.*)

CHANG   Child, how could you be so foolish as to think of such a thing!   You must on no account do that.

HSI-ERH   Aunty, I...I can't face people any more.

CHANG   I understand.   It's my fault for not looking after you better.

HSI-ERH   Aunty, I can't go on living....

CHANG   Don't talk nonsense, child.   What's done is done, but you have to live anyway.   You're young, child, and there is hope.   I'll look after you, and later on we two will live together.   The day will come when we shall avenge your father.... (*Helps her up, wiping her eyes.*)

(HSI-ERH *remains silent.*)

CHANG   Stop crying now, and come and rest.

(TA-SHENG *enters.*)

TA-SHENG   Hung-hsi, Hung-hsi!(*Seeing them.*)   Oh, there you are, Hung-hsi!   Last night you made such trouble, the old lady is asking for you!

(HSI-ERH *looks frightened.*)

CHANG   Go now.

HSI-ERH   Aunty!   (*She clings to* CHANG.)

CHANG   I'll go with you, Hung-hsi.   (*They go out together.*)

(*CURTAIN*)

"Aunty, I . . . I can't face people any more."

ACT III

SCENE I

TIME *Seven months after the Second Act.*
PLACE MRS. HUANG'S *room.*
Enter HUANG *and* MU *carrying wedding invitation cards. The servant* TA-SHENG *follows, holding a teapot; and after him come thugs dressed in military uniform.* CHANG *comes on carrying coloured silk.* MRS. HUANG *enters holding a teacup from which she is sipping. The atmosphere is lively.*

HUANG (*sings*):
  Cassia trees in autumn—
ALL (*sing*):
  Make the whole courtyard fragrant!
HUANG (*sings*):
  Preparing for the wedding —
ALL (*sing*):
  We all work with a will!
MU Our young master is now promoted captain of the militia, and getting married. This is truly a double happiness!
HUANG *and* MRS. HUANG (*sing*):
  The masters are busy!
ALL (*sing*):
  The servants are busy!
  All busy and happy together!

MU The preparations for our master's wedding have made every member of the household happy, whether young or old, master or servant!

MRS. HUANG (*sings*):
New clothes and coverlets must be quickly made!
(CHANG *and* TA-SHENG *tear up the silk, while* HUANG, MRS. HUANG *and* MU *sing cheerfully.*)

TOGETHER (*sing*):
Red silk and green, like ten thousand flowers!

MRS. HUANG (*sings*):
Measure it quickly! Cut it straight!

ALL (*sing*):
Some for our master and some for his bride!
And some for quilts and covers for the bed!
To deck the bride!
To spread the bed!
Let's all hurry to get them made!

MRS. HUANG (*sings*):
Send cards at once to our relatives!

MU (*sings*):
I take my pen and quickly write!

HUANG To Secretary-General Sun of Kuomintang County Headquarters, to Magistrate Liu and Captain Li....

MRS. HUANG To the Seventh Aunt, and to Uncle....

MU (*sings*):
One card is written and then another....

ALL (*sing*):
When the time comes, guests will gather,
Men and women, old and young,
To feast here in our hall together!

MRS. HUANG Chang, go to the servants' quarters, and see how the sewing is getting on.

CHANG Yes, mistress.

MRS. HUANG Ta-sheng, go and see how the preparations for the feast are going forward.

TA-SHENG   Yes, mistress.

MRS. HUANG   Old Mu, you speed them all up.

MU   Yes, mistress.

ALL (*sing*):
> *Cassia trees in autumn make the whole courtyard*
> *   fragrant,*
> *The whole household's busy preparing for the*
> *   wedding!*
> *We're just waiting for the happy day to come,*
> *When with flutes and cymbals we welcome the*
> *   bride home!*

(MU, CHANG *and* TA-SHENG *leave.*)

MRS. HUANG (*in a low voice*)   Son, has that procurer from the city arrived?

HUANG   Not yet.   I'm so worried, yesterday I sent for him again.

MRS. HUANG   Better hurry.   Her condition is more obvious every day, and your wedding is drawing near.   If you don't make haste, and word gets out, our family reputation will be ruined.

HUANG   How about this, Mother—for the next day or two let Old Mu keep an eye on her, and stop her running around.   Later we can find a quiet place, and lock her up.

MRS. HUANG (*approvingly*)   Good. (*Exeunt.*)
    (*Enter* MU.)

MU (*picking up the invitations and glancing round prior to going out again*)   Ah, here comes Hung-hsi. Landlord Huang told me to keep an eye on her. Let's see what she's up to.... (*Hides behind the door.*)

    (*Enter* HSI-ERH, *carrying a wooden pail. She is seven months pregnant, looks haggard, and walks with difficulty.*)

HSI-ERH (*sings*):
> *Seven months have passed—*

Like a twig crushed beneath a stone,
I bear the shame, swallowing my tears.
I can't say how ill I feel.
Things have gone so far, there's no help for me,
I'll just have to bear it and swallow my pride.

(*Entering the room she sees the red silk and invitation cards on the table.*)

HSI-ERH   Ah, there's going to be a wedding. Does it mean Landlord Huang?...

(MU *coughs.* HSI-ERH *steps aside.* *Enter* MU.)

MU   Oh, Hung-hsi, what are you doing here?

HSI-ERH   Fetching hot water for the old lady.

MU   You must be happy now. What do you think I'm doing?

HSI-ERH   How should I know?

MU   Well, look at this! (*Picking up the invitation cards.*)   What are these?

HSI-ERH   Those?

MU   Wedding cards, for the wedding! Ah, these days we're all busy preparing, didn't you know? As for you... you ought to be pleased now! You ought to be laughing! The old lady says you mustn't run around these days.... Just wait! (*Exit.*)

HSI-ERH   What? Steward Mu said I....

(*Enter* HUANG.)

HSI-ERH (*seeing* HUANG)   Oh, it's you.

HUANG   Ah, Hung-hsi! (*Wants to turn back.*)

HSI-ERH (*stopping him*)   You—wait! I want to ask you something....

HUANG   Well, but I'm busy now, Hung-hsi....

HSI-ERH   Let me ask you—

HUANG   All right. (*Taking up an invitation card, and listening helplessly.*)

HSI-ERH   I'm growing bigger every day, what can I do? People laugh at me and despise me. But I

can't die, however much I want to. Tell me, how
shall I live on?...

HUANG Er.... (*Wanting to make off.*)

HSI-ERH (*stopping him*) Sir, you.... (*Weeps.*)

HUANG Now, Hung-hsi, don't cry. Er, you know,
Hung-hsi, the time has nearly come. Just keep
calm. Keep quiet, Hung-hsi, and don't run about.
I'm going now to make preparations. (*Exit hastily.*)
    (*Enter* CHANG *with silk.*)

HSI-ERH (*bewildered*) Aunty....

CHANG So you're here.

HSI-ERH What's that you're carrying, Aunty?

CHANG Clothes I made for the bride.

HSI-ERH Is there going to be a wedding, Aunty?

CHANG I was just going to talk to you, Hung-hsi.
Come along to our room for a talk....
    (*She leads* HSI-ERH *out of the door, to their own
room. The back curtain falls.*)

HSI-ERH Aunty—

CHANG You know, Hung-hsi, the time is getting
near....

HSI-ERH I know.

CHANG You ought to realize.

HSI-ERH I do realize, Aunty: it's seven months now.
But what can I do? At least now he's....

CHANG (*surprised*) What are you talking about,
Hung-hsi?

HSI-ERH Just now Landlord Huang said he was going
to marry me....

CHANG What! You're dreaming, Hung-hsi! You've
got it wrong, child!

HSI-ERH (*greatly taken aback*) What do you mean,
Aunty?

CHANG (*sings*):
    Oh, Hung-hsi, you foolish child,
    He's not going to marry you,

But a girl called Chao from town;
Her family's rich and powerful....
Child!

Just think, Hung-hsi, how could he dream of marrying a servant like you or me?

HSI-ERH   No need to go on, Aunty.   I lost my head for a moment.   Landlord Huang is my enemy; even if he married me, he would make me lead a wretched life.   Oh, it's just because I'm getting bigger every day, and can't do anything about it.   So I thought—

CHANG   Ah, I meant once the child was born you should give it to me to bring up for you; then one day when you left the Huang family you could marry someone else.   I didn't think to tell you about the wedding.   Who could imagine you would suppose....

HSI-ERH   I understand now, Aunty.   Now he's going to be married, and he's cheating me too.   What a devil he is!   I'm not a child.   He's ruined me, so that I can't hold up my head again; but I'm not like my father!   Even a chicken will struggle when it's killed, and I'm a human being!   Even if it kills me, Aunty, I'm going to speak my mind!

CHANG (*crying*)   I never thought of you as a child, love.   I like your spirit—

HSI-ERH   Aunty! (*Too moved to speak she falls into* CHANG'S *arms.*)

   (*Voice offstage:*   "Aunty Chang, the mistress wants you.")

CHANG   Someone's calling me.   Wait a little, Hung-hsi.   I'll be back soon.   (*Crossing the threshold she turns back.*)   Don't go out again.   (*Exit, closing the door.*)

   (HSI-ERH *watches* CHANG *go.   Presently she can no longer contain herself for anger, and rushes out, just as* HUANG *enters from the other side.*)

HSI-ERH (*fiercely*) Sir!

HUANG (*startled*) Hung-hsi, why are you here?

HSI-ERH (*stepping forward*) Sir, you....

HUANG Now, Hung-hsi, go back quickly. It doesn't look good if you're seen in the courtyard.

HSI-ERH (*loudly*) Landlord Huang!

HUANG (*startled*) What! You—

HSI-ERH On New Year's Eve you forced my dad to commit suicide! On New Year's Day you got me to your home. Since I came you've never treated me as a human being, but as dirt beneath your feet! Your mother beats and curses me! (*Coming nearer.*) And you—you ruined me!

HUANG You...why bring that up now?

HSI-ERH (*coming nearer*) I'm seven months gone, but you're getting married and deceiving me! I ask you, what do you mean by it! (*Bites and tears at him.*)

HUANG (*throwing* HSI-ERH *down*) You fool! Mad! (*He shakes her off and hurries out.*)

HSI-ERH (*getting up*) I'll have it out with you! I'll have it out with you! (*Runs out after him.*)

(*CURTAIN*)

SCENE II

MRS. HUANG'S *room.* HUANG *enters hastily.*

HUANG Mother! Mother!

MRS. HUANG (*putting down her opium pipe*) What is it, son?

HUANG Mother, I was too careless. I didn't have Hung-hsi watched, and now she's making trouble.

MRS. HUANG (*sitting on the bed*) What's she been doing?

HUANG She's after me now! Look, Mother, she's coming here! The guests will be here directly. If this gets known, it will be too bad.

MRS. HUANG The fool! She must be mad! Well, you go. Send Old Mu here.

(*Exit* HUANG.)

(MRS. HUANG *picks up a broomstick and stands waiting angrily.* HSI-ERH *runs in.*)

HSI-ERH I'll have it out with you!... (*Enters the room.*)

MRS. HUANG Silly girl! You are mad! Kneel down!

HSI-ERH You! (*Refusing to kneel.*)

MRS. HUANG (*fiercely*) Kneel down!

(HSI-ERH *looks at her angrily, trembling with hate.*)

MRS. HUANG Wretched girl! Do you admit your guilt? I ask you, who got you with child?

HSI-ERH What!

MRS. HUANG Wretched girl! Carrying on with men, you've spoiled our family's reputation. Speak! Who is your lover? Speak up, who is it?

(MU *comes in behind* HSI-ERH'S *back.*)

HSI-ERH (*loudly*) It's your son! (CHANG *is listening from one corner and* HUANG *from another.*)

MRS. HUANG (*furiously*) What! You liar! You are accusing my son? You are asking for trouble! (*Steps forward to strike her.*)

HSI-ERH (*starts to rush forward but is seized by* MU. *She shrieks*) It's your son! It's your son! You've ruined my whole family! There isn't one good person in your Huang family! Not a single man or woman in your family for generations has been any good! You're all bitches and....

MRS. HUANG   Old Mu! Old Mu! Stop her mouth, quickly!

(MU *gags* HSI-ERH *with a handkerchief.*)

MRS. HUANG   Quickly shut her in the inner room and whip her!

(MU *drags* HSI-ERH *to the inner room and whips her. The strokes of the lash and muffled cries are heard.*)

MRS. HUANG   (*listening*) Good, good. Today she must be well beaten.

(CHANG *listens in distress outside the door.*)
(*There is a pause.*)

MRS. HUANG   (*taking out a lock*) Old Mu, lock the door for me.

(*As* MU *locks the door* HUANG *enters hastily.* CHANG *hides herself and listens at the door.*)

HUANG   Mother, it's time now. I think we'll have to find a way to get rid of her. The guests will soon be here. If outsiders hear of this, it will be too bad.

MRS. HUANG   You're right. The bride is coming. If the bride's family hears of it we'll be in an awkward position.... Old Mu, is there anybody outside?

(*As* MU *looks outside the door* CHANG *hides herself.* MU *re-enters the room, closing the door, and* CHANG *listens again.*)

MU   No one.

MRS. HUANG   Good. We mustn't lose any time. To-night when they are all asleep, Old Mu, you get a horse and take her away.

HUANG   Yes, Old Mu. When you get to the city, take the girl to the procurer for him to get rid of quickly. On no account must people know.

MU   Very good, sir. I'll do that. (*Exit.*)

HUANG   Don't be angry, Mother. Let's go to inspect the preparation of the bridal chamber. (*Takes his mother's arm to help her out.*)

(CHANG *hides herself as* HUANG *and* MRS. HUANG *leave. Then she runs into the room and tries to open the inner door, but finds it locked.*)

CHANG   The key? (*She looks for the key on* MRS. HUANG'S *bed, and finding it opens the door. A voice is heard offstage:* "Aunty Chang!" *Enter* TA-SHENG. CHANG *hides the key, and pretends nothing is amiss.*)

TA-SHENG   Aunty Chang! (*He comes in.*) Oh, there you are, Aunty Chang. The mistress wants you to go to supervise the sewing.

CHANG   All right, I'm coming. (TA-SHENG *goes out, followed by a distracted* CHANG.)

(*Voices are heard offstage*):

MU   Old Kao, what a drunkard you are!

KAO   It's the young master's wedding. Why shouldn't I drink?

MU   Saddle a horse for me at once. Quickly!

KAO   Why do you want a horse so late?

MU   Never you mind. Just get it ready.

KAO   All right. All right.

(CHANG *re-enters, carrying cakes, and hastily closes the door. She puts the cakes on the table, then opens the door of the inner room.*)

CHANG   Hung-hsi! Hung-hsi! (*After dragging* HSI-ERH *out, she locks the door and puts the key back on the bed.*)

CHANG   Hung-hsi! (*Undoing the rope binding* HSI-ERH'S *arms.*) Hung-hsi! Hung-hsi! (*Removing the gag from her mouth.*) Hung-hsi! Wake up, Hung-hsi!

HSI-ERH   (*coming to herself*) Who are you?

CHANG   (*softly*) It's Aunty.

HSI-ERH   Ah, Aunty!... (*Falls on* CHANG.)

CHANG Hung-hsi, Hung-hsi, I know all that happened. (*Helping her up.*) You must go quickly. They want to ruin you.

HSI-ERH Ah!

CHANG They're murderers! They've sold you! They'll be coming to fetch you, you must go at once! If you fall into their hands, you'll never escape again.

HSI-ERH Aunty, they...they.... (*She wants to rush out.*)

CHANG (*pulling her back*) Don't be foolish, Hung-hsi. You're no match for them. Go quickly. You must fly for your life.

(HSI-ERH *says nothing.*)

CHANG Go by the back door. Along the gully. I've opened the door for you. Quick! (*They start out.*)

(*Voice from offstage:* "Aunty Chang! Aunty Chang!" *Taking fright they hide. The voice grows fainter.*)

CHANG (*urgently*) Hung-hsi, soon you won't be with me any more. In future you'll have to make up your own mind. I can't go with you. They're calling me.

HSI-ERH Aunty!

CHANG (*giving* HSI-ERH *the cakes from the table*) Here are some cakes to eat on the road. Mind you only drink running water. However hard life is, you have to go on living. Remember how they destroyed your family. A day will come when you can avenge yourself.

HSI-ERH I shall remember, Aunty.

CHANG (*giving* HSI-ERH *money*) Here's some money I've saved. You'll need it on your journey. Soon I'll be leaving their family. One day we shall meet again.

HSI-ERH (*takes the money and kneels down*) Aunty—

CHANG Ah, Hung-hsi, get up. Go quickly. (*Opens the door and runs out, leading* HSI-ERH.)

(*Voice from offstage:* "Aunty Chang! Aunty Chang!")

(*After a while* CHANG *comes back by the way she went out, walking calmly. The third watch sounds. Enter* HUANG *and* MU.)

HUANG (*taking the key from his mother's bed, unlocks the inner room, goes in, and discovers* HSI-ERH *has gone. In surprise*) What! Where's Hung-hsi? She's disappeared!

MU What!

HUANG Old Mu, Hung-hsi has escaped! The back window is open. She must have climbed out through the window. Go and catch her, Old Mu. When you've caught her, strangle her with a rope and throw her into the river, so we won't have any more trouble.

(*They leave the room.*)

MU She won't dare leave by the front gate, sir. Let's go by the back gate. (*Exeunt.*)

(*CURTAIN*)

SCENE III

HSI-ERH *is escaping by the back gate. There are stars in the sky.*

HSI-ERH (*falls down and gets up again. Sings*):
    They want to kill me, to murder me,
    But I've escaped from their tigers' den!
    Mother bore me, Dad brought me up,

I want to live, I want to live!
(*She runs off.*)
(HUANG *and* MU *enter in pursuit, carrying ropes.*)

HUANG   Hurry up after her, Old Mu!

MU   Right.

HUANG   If she took this road, there's a big river in front, and she can't get away.

(*They pursue. A mountain looms in front. On one side is a rushing river flanked by marshland.* HSI-ERH *hurries in.*)

HSI-ERH (*sings*):
I'm going on, I'll not turn back,
I've been wronged and I want revenge!
They killed my dad and ruined me,
I'll remember it in my grave!
(*The sound of running water is heard.*)
I can hear running water,
There's a river gleaming under the stars;
It's a great river flowing east,
I've lost my way—where shall I go?
(*Suddenly the sound of heavy footsteps behind throws her into a panic.*)   Ah! I'm being followed!
(*She stumbles and falls in the mud. When she extricates herself her shoes have fallen off; but her pursuers are near, and she has no time to pick up her shoes.*)   There are some reeds.   I'd better hide myself there.   (*She crawls into the reeds.*)

(*Enter* HUANG *and* MU.)

HUANG   Can you see her, Old Mu?

MU   No. (*They search.*)

HUANG   The river's in front.   Where could she have gone?

MU   The mountains on both sides are steep, and there's no path.

HUANG   A girl, and so near her time, where can she go?

MU   She won't get away, sir. (*They search again.*)

MU (*suddenly discovering a shoe*)   Ah, sir, isn't this Hung-hsi's shoe?

HUANG (*taking the shoe*)   Yes, it's hers alright.

MU   Then she must have jumped into the river.

HUANG   Ah, well, she brought it on herself. Well, that saves us trouble. Let's go back, Old Mu. If questions are asked, we'll just say she stole things and ran away. Don't let anyone know the truth.

MU   Right. (*They leave by the way they came.*)

HSI-ERH (*emerges from the reeds and sings*):
> *They want to kill me, how blind they are!*
> *I'm water that can't be drained dry!*
> *I'm fire that can't be quenched!*
> *I'm not dying, I'm going to live!*
> *And live to be avenged!*
> (*She hurries into the mountains.*)

(*CURTAIN*)

ACT IV

SCENE I

Three years later—the autumn of 1937.
On the hillside overlooking the river, not far from
the Goddess' Temple. It is dusk. The sun is set-
ting.
Enter UNCLE CHAO *with a long whip, leading his flock.*

CHAO (*sings*):
 Year after year passes,
 And the road's overgrown with wild grass;
 Houses crumble and the place is empty,
 Some have died and some have gone.
 When cold winds blow, the lonely grieve;
 Water flows eastward never to return.
 (*He stands at the river's edge watching the water*
 flow eastward, then speaks with feeling.) Ah, how
quickly time passes. It's three years since that
child Hsi-erh drowned herself in the river.... (*Sits*
on a boulder.)
 (*Enter* LI *from one side carrying incense.*)
LI (*seeing* CHAO) Ah, Uncle Chao, watching the flock?
CHAO Well, Li, where are you off to?
LI I'm going to burn incense before the White-haired
 Goddess.
CHAO Burn incense before the White-haired Goddess?
 ... Oh, yes, it's the fifteenth of the moon again
 today....

LI (*sitting down beside* CHAO) It's quite some time now since the White-haired Goddess appeared in these parts....

CHAO Well, we shall see. Something must be going to happen.... (*Leans forward a little, as if he heard something.*)

LI (*suddenly standing up*) Listen, Uncle Chao!

CHAO (*after a pause*) Oh, it's only the wind in the reeds.

LI (*relaxing. Softly*) Tell me, Uncle, have you seen it?

CHAO Seen what?

LI The White-haired Goddess, Uncle. Old Liu met her once in Uncle Yang's land, and Chang Szu saw her when he was cutting wood in the North Mountain gully. They say she was all white, in the shape of a woman; but she was gone in a flash.... (*Shivers.*)

(*Pause.*)

CHAO (*thinking back*) Ah, if the White-haired Goddess were any good, then Hsi-erh's family should have been avenged.

LI May the fairy help us! (*Pauses.*) Say, Uncle, wasn't it that autumn Aunty Chang sent Hsi-erh....

(CHAO *hastily stops him and looks around.*)

LI (*in a lowered voice*) Didn't you say Aunty Chang sent her away?

CHAO Ah, how could a girl run far? She drowned herself in the river, poor thing....

LI (*sighs. They are silent. He looks at the sky*) Uncle, I must go to burn incense now. A storm is coming. (*He moves toward the temple.*)

CHAO (*sighs sadly. Sings*):

Is there no good judge
To right the wrongs of old?
What we suffered in the past

No words can tell!
But if the goddess were any good at all,
She'd avenge the ghosts of those unjustly killed!
(AUNTY WANG, *leaning on* AUNTY CHANG'S *arm,*
enters from the direction of the temple.)

CHANG   Uncle Chao!

CHAO   Oh, Aunty Chang, Aunty Wang!   You've been all that way to burn incense?

CHANG   Well, Aunty Wang insisted I come with her. Ah, when you're brooding over something, you can't forget it.

WANG (*crying*)   Uncle Chao... I want nothing else, great goddess, but let my child come back.... I've never done a bad deed in my life.   Why should this have happened to me?   All these years have passed, Uncle Chao, yet every day as soon as I close my eyes, I see Hsi-erh on one side and Ta-chun on the other. Oh, son, why have you forgotten your mother?   Poor children!   One drowned herself, and the other ran away.... (*Cries bitterly.*)

CHANG   Now don't cry, Aunty Wang. (*Comforting her.*) Don't take on so, Aunty Wang.

CHAO   Nothing can bring the dead to life.   What's the use of crying?...   Although Hsi-erh died, she died well....   As for Ta-chun, although there's been no news of him since he left, he'll come back some day....

CHANG   That's right.   Every day since I left the Huang family, I've reasoned with her, saying, "Wait, Aunty.   Although Hsi-erh is dead, Ta-chun is sure to come back.   Don't complain of fate.   Our fate is the same.   I'll help you, and you help me.   Then we shall struggle along in spite of difficulties."

CHAO (*nodding sadly*)   Struggle along, struggle along. One day Heaven will stop being blind.

(LI *enters hurriedly, in consternation. There is a gust of wind.*)

LI (*looking pale*)   Uncle Chao!   Uncle Chao!

CHAO   What is it?

LI   She's coming!   She's coming!

THE OTHERS   What is it?

LI   Behind the temple!   White!   All white!   The White-haired Goddess!

THE OTHERS (*panic-stricken*)   What, is it true?   Let's go quickly!

(*They run off.* CHAO *follows with his sheep. The sky grows dark, thunder rolls and the storm breaks.*)

(*A chorus sings offstage*):
The storm is coming,
The storm is coming,
THE STORM IS COMING!
Heaven and earth grow dark
With lightning and with thunder!
Heaven and earth grow dark
With lightning and with thunder!
God has grown angry,
And the world's in chaos!
A gale has sprung up, and from the mountain
The White-haired Goddess is coming down!

(*A great clap of thunder and flash of lightning.*)

(*Enter the* WHITE-HAIRED GODDESS—HSI-ERH— *with dishevelled white hair, rushing through the storm.*)

HSI-ERH (*sings*):
I came down to gather fruit and berries,
When this sudden thunderstorm broke.
The mountain's steep and the path is slippery,
I can't get back to my cave, so I'll take shelter
In the Goddess' Temple nearby.

(*She slips and falls, and her fruit rolls to the ground. She hastily picks it up.*)   I've spent more

than three years out of the sun. Today I came out
to get some maize and potatoes, and steal some food
from the shrine for my winter store....

(*Thunder and a downpour.* HSI-ERH *sings*) :
Lightning makes me close my eyes,
Thunder makes me lower my head,
Wind tries to sweep me off my feet,
And I'm drenched in the pouring rain!
But never mind the thunder and lightning,
The wind and the pouring rain!
I clench my teeth
And step by step
Push on—
The temple's close ahead!
(*Exit in the direction of the temple.*)
(MU *enters running through the storm with a*
lantern and umbrella.)

MU (*sings*) :
Thunder's crashing, lightning's flashing,
This storm broke out of the blue!
Master went to town on business,
What's keeping him so long?

(*At a clap of thunder he crouches down.*) Ah,
what weather!... Really, what is the world coming
to! Recently I heard the Japanese fought their way
across from Lukouchiao and have occupied Paoting.
They may even be here in a few days. Landlord
Huang went to town for news. He ought to be back
by now.... (*He is restless and anxious. Thunder*
rolls again. He stares ahead, not knowing what to
do.) Ah, during the last few years the villagers
have been talking about some white-haired goddess,
and ghostly noises are heard at midnight. (*Sighs.*)
What can I do?... (*Shivers.*)

(*He suddenly sees a shadowy figure on the left,*
and gives a start.) Who is it?

(*After a pause,* LANDLORD HUANG'S *voice is heard in the dark:* "Oh.... Is it Old Mu?")

MU (*reassured*)　You're back at last, sir!

(HUANG *hurries in holding an umbrella, followed by* TA-SHENG.)

MU　Are you all right, sir?

HUANG　Things look bad, Old Mu!　(*Sings*):

> *I set out for the county town*
> *The day before yesterday;*
> *But I'd only reached the market town*
> *When I heard some dreadful news!*
> *The Japanese have taken the county town,*
> *So I hurried right back,*
> *Hurried back like mad today!*

MU (*startled*)　What!　Is it true?

TA-SHENG　Yes.

HUANG　It's appalling!　The Japanese kill people and set fire to houses!　All my in-laws have fallen into their hands!

MU (*more alarmed*)　Heavens!　Then what can we do, sir?

HUANG (*reassuringly*)　Don't worry, Old Mu. Whatever changes take place, we'll always be able to find a way out.　Come on, let's go home first.

(*There is a clap of thunder, and the rain pours down more heavily.*)

MU　The storm's growing worse, sir. Let's take shelter first in the temple.　(*The three battle their way toward the temple. On the way they meet* HSI-ERH. *A flash of lightning lights up the* WHITE-HAIRED GODDESS.)

HUANG (*panic-stricken*)　What!

(*There is another flash of lightning, and* HSI-ERH *recognizes* HUANG.)

HUANG　Ghosts!　Ghosts!

(*The three men hide in terror.*)

HSI-ERH (*in rising anger rushes at* HUANG *and the others, throwing the sacrificial fruit at* HUANG *and shrieking*)   Ah!

HUANG and MU (*flying in terror*)   Help!... Help!... Ghosts!   Ghosts!

    (*They rush off, followed by* TA-SHENG.)

    (*A pause.*)

HSI-ERH (*halting in alarm and uncertainty*)   Ghosts? Ghosts?   (*She looks round, then is silent for a moment.*)   Oh, you mean I'm a ghost?   (*She looks at her hair and clothes.*)   So, I don't look like a human being!   (*Her voice trembles with indignation and grief.*)   This is all your doing, Landlord Huang! You brought me to this!   And you call me a ghost?...

    (*Wind, rain and thunder are heard, and lightning flashes, as* HSI-ERH *sings.*)

I'm Hsi-erh whom you ruined,

I'm not a ghost!

    (*Thunder crashes even closer.*)

...I've lived in a cave for more than three years,

Gritting my teeth for misery;

Hiding by day for fear folk see me,

While at night there are tigers and wolves;

I've only rags and leaves to wear,

Only temple offerings and berries to eat,

So my hair and skin have turned white!

(Accusingly):

I was brought up by parents too,

But now I've come to this pass!

It's all through you, Landlord Huang,

You brought me to this, yet now you call me

A ghost!   All right—

I'm a ghost!

The ghost of someone cruelly killed!

The ghost of someone hounded to death!

I'm going to scratch and pinch you!
I'm going to bite you!
(Shrieks.)
(She rushes headlong into the storm.)
(Lightning and sheets of rain.)
(The chorus sings "The Storm..." offstage, the sound gradually dies away in the distance.)

(CURTAIN)

SCENE II

The following afternoon.
Under a big tree at one end of the village.
OLD CHAO *and two peasants enter. They are obviously upset.*

ALL (sing):
    A storm's sprung up. The world's
    In a bad way, we can't live in peace.
FIRST PEASANT:
    Landlord Huang has practically squeezed us dry!
SECOND PEASANT:
    The White-haired Goddess is making trouble!
CHAO:
    The Japanese are fighting their way over!
PEASANTS:
    It's said they've taken Paoting city!
FIRST PEASANT:
    Hu-tzu has gone to town for news,
SECOND PEASANT:
    Why isn't he back yet?
ALL:
    It's enough to distract one, such goings on!

"Help! . . . Help! . . . Ghosts! Ghosts!"

CHAO Ah, Hu-tzu went to town three days ago; how is it he's not back yet?

FIRST PEASANT Could he have met the Japanese?

SECOND PEASANT Surely they can't be there already? (*Sighs.*)

(*As the three are waiting impatiently,* AUNTY CHANG *hurries in.*)

CHANG Oh, you're here. Have you heard the news?

ALL (*startled*) What's happened?

CHANG Yesterday evening when Landlord Huang was coming back from town and took shelter in the temple from the rain, he saw a ghost!

ALL (*amazed*) Really?

CHANG It's true. He's ill now from the shock.

CHAO Well! Now the Huang family's sins are finding them out, if ghosts come out to confront him!

CHANG And I heard those Japanese have occupied the county town!

ALL (*startled*) No! Then what's to be done?

CHAO (*stamping impatiently*) Why isn't Hu-tzu back yet?

FIRST PEASANT Oh, look! Isn't that Hu-tzu coming?

ALL (*shouting*) Hu-tzu! Hu-tzu!

(HU-TZU *hurries in.*)

HU-TZU (*panting*) You're all here. Things are in a bad way! (*Sings*):
The Japanese have taken the county town,
And smashed the Kuomintang troops!
The county head's fled, the commissioner too,
Leaving just the people, with nowhere to turn!

ALL Ah! Only the people are left to bear the brunt!

HU-TZU (*sings*):
When the Kuomintang troops fled from the
market town,
There was cursing, conscripting, beating and
looting!

And when the Japanese come, so they say,
There's always burning, raping, shooting!

ALL Heavens! Only the people are left with no one to care for them!

HU-TZU (*sings*):
But I heard some good news too—
Troops have come from the west, with banners flying.
They'll fight the Japanese and save us all!
They can march sixty miles in a single night,
They're super men and officers, they really fight!

ALL (*astounded*) Really?

HU-TZU (*sings*):
At Pinghsing Pass they won a great victory,
Killing several thousand Japanese,
Then fought their way north....

ALL What army is that?

HU-TZU (*sings*):
They call it the eight—eight—
Eighth Route Army!

ALL (*at a loss, echoing him*) What—the Eighth Route Army?

HU-TZU (*emphatically*) Yes. They're called the Eighth Route Army. I heard they're very good to the people—

(LI *rushes in before* HU-TZU *has finished, carrying a hoe.*)

(*The "Eighth Route Army March" is heard.*)

LI (*showing amazement*) Quick! Quick! I was just coming in from the fields, when I saw troops coming down the Southern Hill!

ALL (*alarmed*) What! Troops?

FIRST PEASANT Could it be the Japanese?

LI No, they didn't look like Japanese. They're Chinese troops!

SECOND PEASANT Ah, they must be retreating.

LI   They don't look like retreating either.   You look!
(*All stare in the direction he points.*)   They're in
good order, heading briskly due north.

ALL (*looking*)   Ah, there are so many of them!

LI   Ha!   That's a funny army!   They're all youngsters, wearing big straw hats, and with no puttees,
only shoes.   And there's a figure "eight" on their
sleeves.

ALL (*in unison*)   Oh, they must be the Eighth Route
Army!
(*The martial music grows louder.*)
(*They watch anxiously.*)

SECOND PEASANT (*suddenly catching sight of them*)
Ah!   Here they come!   Here they come!
(*An armyman's voice offstage:* "Hey!   Country-
man—countrymen!")
(*They all take cover in fright.*)
(*Enter* TA-SO, *ragged and unkempt, leading a
soldier who proves to be* TA-CHUN.)

TA-SO   By calling out like that, Ta-chun, you frightened them all away!   Say, Ta-chun, just now there
was someone here who looked like Uncle Chao.

TA-CHUN   Let's call him then.

TA-SO   Uncle Chao!   Uncle Chao!

TA-CHUN (*calling too*)   Uncle Chao!
(*After a pause,* CHAO *and others enter; but the
sight of the soldier makes them fall back a few steps
in fear.*)

TA-CHUN (*advancing*)   Uncle Chao, don't you know
me?   I'm Ta-chun!

TA-SO   I'm Ta-so!

ALL (*incredulously*)   What? — Ta-chun! — Ta-so!
(*After a second they recognize them, and are overjoyed.*)   Well!   Well!   Ta-chun!   Ta-so!   You've
come back!   (*Other peasants crowd in.*)
(*They sing happily in unison*):

A clap of thunder,
And then a sunny sky!
The stars in heaven
Are falling from on high!
Ta-chun! (*Some: Ta-so!*) *You've been away so*
    long,
Who could tell you would come home today!

(*Enter a peasant:* "Ta-chun! Your mother's
coming!")

(TA-CHUN *goes to meet her.*)

ALL (*following* TA-CHUN *to meet her, sing*):
Now mother and son will meet,
And be together from now on!
All we country folk are happy too;
All we country folk are happy for you!

(AUNTY WANG, *calling* "Ta-chun! Ta-chun!",
runs in.)

TA-CHUN (*shouts*) Mother!

WANG (*unable to believe her eyes, hesitates, then*
    rushes forward, crying) Ta-chun! My boy!

TA-CHUN Mother! (*He breaks down too.*)

SOME PEASANTS (*comfortingly*) Aunty Wang....
(*Sing*):
Don't take on so!

OTHERS (*sing*):
Don't be so upset, Ta-chun!

CHANG Don't make your mother sad, Ta-chun!

CHAO (*wiping his eyes*) Don't take on so, Aunty.
    Ta-chun's back, isn't he?

WANG (*wiping her eyes*) Oh... I'm not... not sad.
    (*Cries again.*)

CHAO Well! (*Sings*):
You waited day after day so many years,
Now Ta-chun's here, isn't he?

ALL (*sing*):
Isn't it grand that he's back!

CHANG   Your day of rejoicing has come, Aunty.

CHAO   Tell us, Ta-chun, how did you come back?

TA-CHUN and TA-SO   Right!

TA-CHUN   Mother, Uncle—

TA-SO   Aunty Chang, neighbours—

TA-CHUN and TA-SO (*sing*) :

> *When we left that year,*
> *Landlord Huang—*

TA-CHUN:

> *Drove me out with nowhere to go!*

TA-SO:

> *Threw me into the county jail!*

TA-CHUN:

> *I fled to Shansi province,*
> *And joined the army there!*

TA-SO:

> *Life was misery in that jail!*

TA-CHUN:

> *Today our troops have come to the front,*
> *Determined to fight the Japanese invaders!*

TA-SO:

> *They stormed the county town and opened the*
>   *jail doors,*
> *Letting us out after all we'd suffered!*

BOTH:

> *So we came back together,*
> *Home to see our old neighbours!*

ALL (*to* TA-CHUN)   What army do you belong to then?

TA-CHUN (*sings*) :

> *I'm in the Eighth Route Army.*

TA-SO (*simultaneously*) :

> *He's in the Eighth Route Army!*

ALL (*delighted, crowding round him*)   Oh, so you joined the Eighth Route Army then! (*Sing*) :

The Eighth Route Army! The Eighth Route
Army!
You've come from the west!
It was you who won the battle of Pinghsing Pass,
You're the army with the super officers and men!

TA-CHUN   Yes, the Eighth Route Army, led by the
Communist Party, is like one family with the common people. Do you remember, Uncle Chao, you
used to talk about the Red Army? That Red Army
is the present Eighth Route Army!

CHAO   Eh? What's that you say? The Eighth
Route is the same as the Red Army? (*Wildly happy,*
to all.) Ho! Have you all forgotten the Red Army
that came to Chao Village on the thirteenth of the
fifth moon that year, the day the War God sharpened
his knife?.... It's too good to be true! It's too good
to be true! Everything will work out all right
now. The Red Army's come back again!

TA-CHUN   (*correcting him*)   The Eighth Route Army
—the Eighth Route Army's come back!

ALL   (*in unison*)   The Eighth Route Army — the
Eighth Route Army's come back! Now there'll
really be a change for the better!

(*Laughter.*)

(*The "Eighth Route Army March" sounds loudly*
offstage.)

(*All go to meet the troops.*)

(*CURTAIN*)

ACT V

SCENE I

Spring, 1938.

Under the big tree in front of the village. The tree has come into leaf. This village has become one of the Eighth Route Army's anti-Japanese bases behind the enemy's lines. The early morning sun lights up the sentry box of the Self Defence Corps. From a tree beside it hangs a reading board on which is written: "Resist Japan and Reduce Rents."

HU-TZU, *carrying a lance with a red silk tassel, is on sentry duty.*

HU-TZU (*sings*):

    The first clap of thunder in spring!
    The first lamp lit in the valley!
    The poor are going to be masters,
    Now the Communist Party's come!
    We mustn't be afraid, we must fight
    To build up our new people's power.
    Since the government's ordered rents reduced,
    We must all rally round and work hard!

    (*Cheerfully.*) Ah! At last the time has come for us poor folk to be masters! Last year when Ta-chun was transferred here from the army he became assistant officer of our district. When the village held an election for political officers in the first moon, Uncle Chao was elected village head and Ta-so chairman of the Peasants' Union. Now an order has come that rents be reduced, so we shall have to settle old scores with Landlord Huang. (*Sighs.*) Only the villagers don't all see eye to eye yet. Folk are still so afraid of Landlord Huang and that "White-haired Goddess" that nobody dares stick his neck out. There was to be a meeting today, but I'm sure they won't all come. (*Walks to one side to look round.*)

(*Enter* UNCLE CHAO *and* TA-SO.)

CHAO and TA-SO (*sing*):

If everyone rallies round,
Our struggle is sure to succeed!
The government will back us up,
They're sending us cadres today.

TA-SO   Hu-tzu!

HU-TZU (*turning round*) Oh, Ta-so! . . . Oh no— (*Hastily correcting himself.*) Peasant Union Chairman and Village Head. (*Laughs.*)

CHAO (*laughing too*) Have you seen anybody from the district, Hu-tzu?

HU-TZU (*impatiently*) Not yet!

TA-SO They said they'd come today; why aren't they here yet? (*Goes to one side to look.*)

CHAO Hu-tzu! This time we're going to demand rent reduction and settle old scores with Landlord Huang. How about it, youngster, do you dare stand out and speak up?

HU-TZU Need you ask, Village Head? Of course I want to attack Landlord Huang. (*Raising his thumb.*) I'll be the first! . . . But one person isn't enough. See here, this looks bad: a meeting was announced for today, but so far nobody's shown up! Bah! I think it'll be a washout.

CHAO (*reassuringly*) Now, Hu-tzu, don't you worry. It's always darkest before dawn. Today cadres are coming from the district with Ta-chun, we've already thought out a good plan, and we're not afraid of Landlord Huang's tricks!... Keep cool, youngster, and wait and see. It won't be long now!

HU-TZU   All right. (*Smiles contentedly.*)

TA-SO (*seeing figures on the road to the village*)   Hey, Uncle Chao, is that Ta-chun and the district head there?

(CHAO *and* HU-TZU *look.*)

HU-TZU   Yes, it is. It's Ta-chun. And the district head!

(*Two figures approach, and they go eagerly to meet them, calling "District Head!" "Ta-chun!"*)

(*The district head and* TA-CHUN *walk briskly in.*)

HU-TZU   Hey! Ta-chun.... Oh no, it's our Assistant Officer Wang who's come!

(TA-CHUN *mops his head and smiles at* HU-TZU.)

CHAO (*to the district head*)   We've been waiting a long time. Why are you so late?

DISTRICT HEAD (*wiping his face*)   Ta-chun and I came by way of Liu Village, otherwise we'd have been here much earlier.

CHAO   How about it? I suggest we go first to the village office.

TA-SO   Yes, let's go to the village office first.

(*They start for the village.*)

(*Sound of villagers singing in unison offstage.*)

DISTRICT HEAD (*seeing the villagers approaching*)   Hullo! What are these folk doing?

HU-TZU (*stepping forward*)   Bah! They're going again to sacrifice to the "White-haired Goddess," damn them! See, there's that rogue Steward Mu too!

TA-CHUN (*to the district head*)   Suppose we step out of sight for a second, District Head, and watch them?

CHAO Yes, just come over here. (*They hide on one side.* HU-TZU *takes cover too.*)

(*Enter the villagers—an old man, an old woman, two peasants and two women, carrying incense and offerings.* MU *follows.*)

ALL (*sing*):
> The world is out of joint,
> And troubles never cease;
> But the White-haired Goddess has power
> To protect and give us peace!

MU (*seeing there is no one about, addresses them craftily*) Ah, do you know? Another strange thing happened yesterday evening!

ALL (*startled*) What?

MU The White-haired Goddess appeared again!
(*Sings*):
> Yesterday, at the dead of night,
> The White-haired Goddess appeared again!
> "*You shan't reap what you've sown,*" she said.
> There's great trouble ahead!
> Ruin will stalk the land,
> Everywhere men will die,
> Everywhere fires will break out,
> The sound of weeping will reach the sky!

ALL (*aghast*) Oh! What can we do?

MU (*sings*):
> Then she warned men:
> To be safe and sound,
> You must do good deeds!
> Don't meddle in things that aren't your concern,
> And offer more incense in the temple.
> If you do this you'll be safe!

ALL (*pray*) Oh, Goddess, help us!

MU And the goddess said too—(*Sings*):
> The Eighth Route Army won't last long,
> It'll vanish like dew in the sun!

When the sun comes out the dew disappears,
And the Eighth Route Army will soon be gone!
(HU-TZU *has already appeared behind* MU. *Now he rushes forward, snatches* MU'S *incense and candles, and dashes them to the ground.*)

HU-TZU   You bastard, what rumours are you spreading?

MU (*taken by surprise, is at a loss for words*)   I... I.... (*Stoops to pick up his incense and candles.*)

HU-TZU   Get out! (*Kicks him off, stamping on the candles and incense.*)
(*Exit* MU *in alarm.*)
(*The others make as if to leave, but* HU-TZU *stops them.*)

HU-TZU (*angrily*)   Stop! No one must pass! Well! When you are summoned to a meeting you won't come, but you have plenty of time for burning incense.

CROWD (*protestingly*):
What are you doing, Hu-tzu?
What if you offend the goddess?
This concerns us all, not just you.

HU-TZU (*not yielding*)   The goddess, indeed! Where is the goddess? No, I won't let you go! (*He is spoiling for a fight.*)
(*The district head,* TA-CHUN, CHAO *and* TA-SO *come in hastily.* CHAO *pulls* HU-TZU *aside and restrains him.*)

CHAO   Hu-tzu....

TA-SO   Don't be angry. No need to get excited.

DISTRICT HEAD   That's right, friends. Don't get heated....
(*The crowd quietens down.*)

OLD MAN   Now the district head is here.

CROWD   Ah, District Head, Ta-chun....

DISTRICT HEAD Friends, weren't you talking about the White-haired Goddess? Let's hear what miracles the goddess has worked.

TA-CHUN That's right. Just what?

OLD MAN District Head, Ta-chun.... (*Sings*):
The White-haired Goddess often shows herself,
It's three whole years now we've seen her.

FIRST PEASANT (*sings*):
We've all seen her,
She comes and goes without a trace....

SECOND PEASANT She's all in white! A flash—and she's gone! (*Sings*):
She's often in the Goddess' Temple,
Where she comes out at dead of night!

THIRD PEASANT (*sings*):
The sacrifice set out one day
Will be gone by the next!

FOURTH PEASANT (*sings*):
She declares truths in the temple,
Every word can be heard distinctly!

FIFTH PEASANT It's true. She said—(*Sings*):
Men are wicked, sinful creatures,
That's why we can't have peace!

SIXTH PEASANT And Steward Mu told us—(*Sings*):
The White-haired Goddess is so powerful,
We must all mend our ways!

ALL (*sing*):
Otherwise we'll offend her, and that'll be the end of us!

HU-TZU (*impatiently*) That's a pack of lies! Where is the White-haired Goddess? Why haven't I seen her?

(*The crowd shows fresh indignation.*)

FIRST How can you say that, Hu-tzu?

SECOND Everybody knows how powerful the goddess is.

THIRD   Who will bear her anger if you offend her?

DISTRICT HEAD (*intervening persuasively*)   Friends, don't lose your heads.   Let's look into the business of the goddess.   We must get to the bottom of it....   If you want to burn incense, we won't stop you. But I hope you'll give some thought too to the matter of reducing rents.   Our government will always work for the people.

TA-CHUN   Just think what we've suffered all these years.   Now the communists are here, leading us to become our own masters.   We must stand up and act!

OLD MAN   Well, yes, District Head, Ta-chun.... We'll leave you now.

DISTRICT HEAD   All right.   In a few days we'll get together and have a talk. (*The villagers leave.*)

DISTRICT HEAD (*to* CHAO *and* TA-SO)   Village Head, Ta-so, it's clear what's happening.   We've studied the relevant materials in our office too. (*In a low voice.*)   This is no simple matter....

TA-CHUN (*following him up*)   That's right.   Landlord Huang is involved.   The district office has decided to get to the bottom of the mystery of the "White-haired Goddess".... Tonight there'll be a full moon. I think Ta-so and I should go to the Goddess' Temple....

     (*They confer in whispers.*)

DISTRICT HEAD (*to* CHAO *and* TA-SO)   What do you think?   Do you agree?

CHAO   Yes.   A good idea.

TA-SO   Right, let's see what happens tonight.

DISTRICT HEAD   Better be on your guard, Village Head.

CHAO (*eagerly*)   That goes without saying.... (*Turns to* HU-TZU.)   Hu-tzu, you keep a sharp watch in that direction tonight. Our day of vengeance is coming, youngster.

TA-CHUN Then let's go quickly and prepare.

(*They walk briskly out.*)

(HU-TZU, *holding his red-tasselled lance, climbs onto a mound to stand guard.*)

(*CURTAIN*)

SCENE II

Evening.

The Goddess' Temple. There are offerings on the shrine. It is dark and eerie.

Enter TA-CHUN *carrying a pistol, and* TA-SO *with an unlighted torch and a big knife. Approaching the door, they look around, then whisper together and enter the temple.* TA-CHUN *points out a corner to* TA-SO, *and both hide themselves.*

The wind roars. The temple lamp sheds an eerie light. Pause.

TA-CHUN *peers out from the gloom, then shrinks back into the shadows.*

There is musical accompaniment throughout.

TA-SO (*nervously*) Ta-chun! Ta-chun!

TA-CHUN (*stopping him*) Quiet! (*Makes a gesture, and they keep silent again.*)

(*Enter the "White-haired Goddess" from outside. She darts behind the shrine. After a while, seeing there is nobody there, she comes out to collect the sacrifices on the shrine.*)

(TA-CHUN *and* TA-SO *leap out from the darkness.*)

TA-CHUN (*shouting*) Who are you?

HSI-ERH (*taken by surprise, is bewildered. She shrieks and rushes at* TA-CHUN)   Ah!

(TA-CHUN *fires.* HSI-ERH *is hit in the arm and falls, but she gets up and runs out in fright.*)

TA-CHUN   Ta-so! After her, quick!

(*The scene changes.   On the mountain path.*)

(HSI-ERH, *clutching her wounded arm, runs with difficulty, and jumps over a ditch and runs off.*)

(TA-CHUN *and* TA-SO *follow.*)

TA-SO   Which way?   She's vanished again!

TA-CHUN (*looks around and down at the ground*) The trail of blood has disappeared too.

TA-SO (*looking down*)   There's a valley beneath us. We have come a long way.

TA-CHUN (*making a discovery*)   Look, Ta-so! There's a gleam of light!

TA-SO   Ah, it must be a cave!

(*The crying of a child is heard.*)

TA-CHUN (*listening hard*)   There seems to be a child crying.... Let's go after her, Ta-so.

(*The two jump across the ditch.*)

TA-CHUN   Ta-so, light the torch! (*Exeunt.*)

(*The music continues.   There is a gust of wind.*)

(*The scene changes again.   Inside the cave.   An oil lamp gleams on a ledge of the rock, its flickering light revealing the gloom and horror of the cave. On one side are piled firewood, wild fruit, maize and temple offerings.   The child is struggling and crying on the firewood as* HSI-ERH, *panic-stricken, crawls into the cave, and blocks the entrance with a rock.   Seeing its mother the child crawls over, crying "Ma!"   Outside the cave* TA-CHUN'S *voice is heard "Ta-so! Here! Here!"   They push at the rock, which crashes down.   They enter the cave,* TA-SO *holding the torch.* HSI-ERH *hastily steps to one side to shield her child with her body.*)

TA-CHUN (*covering* HSI-ERH *with his pistol*)   Are you man or spirit?   Speak!

TA-SO   Quickly!   Man or spirit?

TA-CHUN   Speak or I'll fire!

HSI-ERH (*with hatred, fiercely*)   I....

TA-CHUN   Speak!   Speak and I'll let you go.

HSI-ERH   I... I.... (*Explosively.*) I'm human, human, human! (*Sings*):

> I'm flesh and blood!   I've a heart like you!
> Why do you say I'm not human?

TA-CHUN   Where did you come from?

HSI-ERH (*sings*):

> Under the mountain a stream flows by,
> From Yangko Village my family!

TA-CHUN and TA-SO (*startled*)   Then how did you come here?

HSI-ERH   All because of your Huang family! (*Sings*):

> You hounded my dad to death!
> You forced Ta-chun to leave home! (TA-CHUN *and*
>   TA-SO *stand dumbfounded.*)
> You want to kill me, but I won't die!
> I came and lived in this cave,
> Each day I traced a line on the stone,
> But they're not enough to express my hate!
> Such hate, such burning for revenge
> Is cut in my bones and engraved on my heart!
> Ah! (*Cries.*)
> Did you think I was dead?
> You were wrong, wrong! (*Laughs loudly.*)
> I'm a fire you'll never put out!
> I'm a tree you'll never uproot!

TA-CHUN and TA-SO   What is your name?

HSI-ERH (*sings*):

> I'm the fire in the waste, I'm the tree on the hill!
> And I am Hsi-erh—who is living still!
> (TA-CHUN *and* TA-SO *exclaim in amazement.*)

HSI-ERH   Well, now you've come again, I'll have it out with you!   I'll have it out with you!   (*Rushes wildly at them.*)   (TA-CHUN *and* TA-SO *stand there at a loss. The torch in* TA-SO'S *hand is still burning, and by its light she sees* TA-CHUN'S *face.*)   Ah, you, you!   (*To her amazement she recognizes* TA-CHUN.)   Are you Ta-chun?   (*Faints.*)

(*The child cries over her.*)

(TA-CHUN *and* TA-SO *step forward hastily and look at her.*)

TA-CHUN   (*speaking as if in a dream*)   Yes....It is Hsi-erh.   (*He pauses, not knowing what to do, then sees the wound on her arm.*)   Ah!   (*Taking a towel, he binds it up very sadly, calling softly.*)   Hsi-erh!

TA-SO   Hsi-erh!

(*The pain of her wound brings* HSI-ERH *to herself. She sighs and opens her eyes.   When she sees* TA-CHUN *she knows all is well, and listlessly closes her eyes again.*)

(*Musical accompaniment.*)

TA-CHUN   (*looks from* HSI-ERH *to the cave.   He remembers all the past, and his tears flow.   Then he grows angry.*)   Now I understand everything!   Ta-so!   Go back quickly to tell the district head.   Have Landlord Huang arrested!   Tell Old Chen to report to the district!

TA-SO   Right!

TA-CHUN   Hold on!   And tell my mother and Aunty Chang to bring some clothes to fetch Hsi-erh back!

TA-SO   Right!   (*Hurries off.*)

TA-CHUN   (*to* HSI-ERH)   Hsi-erh!   Hsi-erh!   (HSI-ERH *comes to herself.*)   We've come to ask you to go back.

HSI-ERH   Eh?   To go back?   (*Shakes her head.*)

TA-CHUN   (*vehemently*)   You don't realize, Hsi-erh, how things have changed outside.   Do you remem-

ber the Red Army Uncle Chao spoke about that year?
Well, now the Red Army's come—it's called the
Eighth Route Army now. They've come, and we
poor folks have become masters! You must go out,
we must take revenge!

HSI-ERH (*after a pause, in a low voice*) Ah...
changed... changed! Revenge! (*She nods.*) Revenge!

(TA-CHUN *takes off his jacket and puts it over*
HSI-ERH'S *shoulders, then picks up the child and
leads* HSI-ERH *out of the cave. Dawn is breaking
and birds can be heard. There is sunlight outside
the cave.*)

(*Singing offstage*):
The sun's come out! The sun's come out!
The sun so bright—a blaze of light!
For generations till today
We suffered pain and grief;
But today we've seen the sun rise
To drive away the gloom of night!
Where did our Hsi-erh disappear to?
She's left us many a year.
But today—
We'll trample down the hill,
We'll tear open the mountain cave,
To rescue Hsi-erh!
To rescue her!

(TA-SO *leads the district head,* AUNTY WANG,
AUNTY CHANG, OLD CHAO *and others up the mountain path. They enter singing.*)

ALL (*sing*):
Where is Hsi-erh?
Where is Hsi-erh?

TA-SO Over there—ah, look!

ALL (*sing*):
Hsi-erh has come! She's coming home!

(*They advance in welcome.*)

(HSI-ERH'S *appearance dumbfounds them.* After *a moment* AUNTY WANG *goes up to her.*)

WANG   Hsi-erh!

CHANG (*going to her*)   Hsi-erh!

CHAO   Hsi-erh!

(*Seeing these familiar faces,* HSI-ERH *is at first unable to speak.* Presently she calls: "Uncle Chao! Aunty Chang! Aunty Wang!" *Finally she falls into* AUNTY WANG'S *arms and sobs bitterly.* All *are moved to tears.* AUNTY WANG *and* AUNTY CHANG *straighten* HSI-ERH'S *hair.*)

DISTRICT HEAD   Don't be sad, friends! Today we've rescued Hsi-erh! That's good! Tomorrow we'll hold a mass meeting to accuse Landlord Huang, avenge Hsi-erh and vent our anger. Let's go back now!

ALL (*sing*):
  Country folk, comrades, don't shed tears!
  The old life forced men to turn into ghosts,
  But the new life changes ghosts back into men,
  It's saved our unhappy sister here!
  The new life changes ghosts into men,
  She's been restored to us again!
  (*While singing they help* HSI-ERH *off.*)

(*CURTAIN*)

SCENE III

The following morning at sunrise.
At the gate of the HUANG *family ancestral hall, chosen as the meeting place for the peasants' mass meeting.*

Gongs sound offstage. Shouts are heard: "Come to
the meeting!" "The meeting's at the gate of the
Huang family ancestral hall."

(*Singing offstage*):
Age-old injustice must be avenged,
And a thousand years' wrongs be set right!
Hsi-erh, who was forced to become a ghost,
Becomes human again today!
Crushing rents must be reduced,
The grain extorted must be restored!
Those who suffered their whole lives long,
Will stand up and become the masters today!

How much of our blood have you sucked?
How much have you drunk of our sweat?
How much of our grain did you steal?
How much of our gold did you get?
How long have you tricked and oppressed us?
How many deaths lie at your door?
Today we shall settle scores with you,
Settle every old score!

(*The curtain parts.*)

(*Innumerable peasants have stood up to accuse*
LANDLORD HUANG.)

(*The district head,* TA-CHUN, UNCLE CHAO *and*
others are standing on the platform. Self Defence
Corps guards, armed with red-tasselled lances and
swords, surround the meeting place. LANDLORD
HUANG, *in mourning for his mother, stands with*
bent head below the platform, while STEWARD MU
has hidden under the table.)

(HUANG *has just spoken, and now it is the turn*
of the masses to question him. Feeling is running
high.)

FIRST PEASANT (*sings*):
>   *You pretend to reduce the rent, but it's all a lie!*

ALL (*in chorus*):
>   *You pretend to reduce the rent, but it's all a lie!*

SECOND PEASANT (*sings*):
>   *You take the land back on the sly!*

ALL (*in chorus*):
>   *You take the land back on the sly!*

THIRD PEASANT (*sings*):
>   *When you've rumours to spread, you rattle away!*

ALL (*in chorus*):
>   *When you've rumours to spread, you rattle away!*

FOURTH PEASANT (*sings*):
>   *When you hound folk to death, you've nothing to
>   say!*

ALL (*in chorus*):
>   *Then you've nothing to say!*
>   *Then you've nothing to say!*
>   *So much rent you squeezed, so much money too,*
>   *There's no counting the tragedies caused by you!*
>   Speak, Landlord Huang!   Speak up, you!

(HUANG *mumbles and wants to justify himself.
   The crowd grows angry.*)

CHAO (*sings*):
>   *Landlord Huang, do you argue still?*
>   *To pretend to be crazy will serve you ill!*

ALL (*in chorus*):
>   *Serve you ill!*

TA-CHUN   Landlord Huang, I tell you—(*Sings*):
>   *The bad old times have got to stop!*
>   *We common folk are up on top!*

ALL (*in chorus*):
>   *Today the world is ours instead!*
>   *Murderers must atone for the dead!*
>   *Pay what you owe to the folk you've bled!*
>   *We'll have your blood for the blood you've shed!*

(Two peasant women rush forward.)

FIRST WOMAN (*sings*) :
  That year—in the ninth moon,
SECOND WOMAN (*simultaneously*) :
  That year—in the twelfth moon,
FIRST WOMAN (*sings*) :
  You came to our door for the rent!
SECOND WOMAN (*simultaneously*) :
  You came to our door for the debt!
FIRST WOMAN (*sings*) :
  You beat my boy till he nearly died!
SECOND WOMAN (*simultaneously*) :
  You beat my dad till you broke his legs!
TOGETHER (*sing*) :
  We'll have your blood for the blood you've shed!
ALL (*sing*) :
  Murderers must atone for the dead!
  Pay what you owe to the folk you've bled!
  We'll have your blood for the blood you've shed!
  (THIRD and FOURTH PEASANTS rush forward.)
THIRD PEASANT (*sings*) :
  The wrong you did me I'll never forget!
FOURTH PEASANT (*simultaneously*) :
  The hatred I bear you I'll never forget!
THIRD PEASANT (*sings*) :
  My son must repair the dike, you said!
FOURTH PEASANT (*sings*) :
  My brother must build you a tower, you said!
  My brother fell to his death from the tower!
THIRD PEASANT (*sings*) :
  My son was swept off and drowned in the flood!
TOGETHER (*sing*) :
  Your crimes will be visited on your head!
ALL (*sing*) :
  Murderers must atone for the dead!
  Pay what you owe to the folk you've bled!

We'll have your blood for the blood you've shed!
(*The crowd roars*):
Make Landlord Huang speak!
Landlord Huang!   Answer us!
(HUANG *continues to mutter.*)

CHAO (*loudly*)   Neighbours!   Since he won't confess,
let's not waste our breath on him!   Hu-tzu!   You
fetch Hsi-erh here!

ALL (*echoing him*)   Right!   Fetch Hsi-erh!
(HU-TZU *runs off.*   HUANG *and* MU *stand aghast.*)

PEASANT WOMEN (*tearfully, sing*):
Hsi-erh! . . .

ANOTHER GROUP OF WOMEN (*sing*):
Hsi-erh! . . .

PEASANTS (*sing*):
Hsi-erh! . . .
Hsi-erh! . . .

PEASANT WOMEN (*sing*):
The poor child suffered bitterly,
But a new life starts for us poor folk today!

ALL (*sing*):
A new life starts!   A new life starts today!
(HU-TZU'S *voice offstage:* "Hsi-erh is coming!")
(*All turn to see* HSI-ERH. *Sing*):
Today the world belongs to us,
We'll take revenge for past wrongs!
Past wrongs!
We'll accuse!
We'll accuse!
And avenge Hsi-erh for all past wrongs!
(*Enter* AUNTY WANG *and* AUNTY CHANG *sup-*
porting HSI-ERH, *who is wearing a new dress.*)

THE CROWD (*shouts*)   We want vengeance for Hsi-erh!
(*Seeing* HUANG, HSI-ERH *rushes across like a mad*
thing to scratch him, but her thirst for vengeance
overcomes her, so that she falls fainting into the

arms of AUNTY WANG *and* AUNTY CHANG.)
　　(*Pause.*)

CHAO (*moved to tears*)　Child, don't be upset!　The
　　time has come for you to speak!

TA-CHUN　Hsi-erh!　Did you hear?　The time has
　　come for you to speak!

HSI-ERH (*as if in a dream*)　What? The time...has
　　come...for us to speak?

ALL (*thunderously*)　Yes! Hsi-erh, the time has come
　　to speak!

WANG and CHANG　Speak, child!

HSI-ERH　I'll speak, I'll speak, I—will—speak!
　　(*Sings*):

> *I want vengeance for all that happened,*
> *My wrongs are too many to tell!*
> *They're a mountain that can't be levelled,*
> *A sea that can't be drained!*
> *But what's caused such a great change*
> *That I can beard my enemy today?*
> *Landlord Huang—*
> *To be cut into pieces is too good for you!*

ALL (*sing*):

> *To be cut into pieces is too good for you!*
> *To be cut into pieces is too good for you!*
> *To be cut into pieces is too good for you!*

HSI-ERH (*sings*):

> *That year—(Her voice falters.)*

WANG (*sings*):

> *That year on New Year's Eve,*

HSI-ERH (*sings*):

> *In storm and snow—*

WANG (*sings*):

> *Mu came and pressed for rent!*

HSI-ERH (*sings*):

> *And hounded my dad to death!*

WANG (*sings*):
> Our good Old Yang was hounded to death!

ALL (*sing*):
> Those hounded to death
> Are too many to count!
> Too many to count!

HSI-ERH (*sings*):
> On New Year's Day—

CHANG (*sings*):
> They took her to the Huangs' house that day—

HSI-ERH (*sings*):
> I led a wretched life there—

CHANG (*sings*):
> She was raped by Landlord Huang!

PEASANT WOMEN (*shocked, sing*):
> Ah! Ah!

HSI-ERH (*cries and sings*):
> Ah!...

CHANG (*sings*):
> Then they wanted to sell her—

HSI-ERH (*sings*):
> As a prostitute!
> Landlord Huang! Landlord Huang!
> Murderous brute!

ALL (*sing*):
> You man-devouring beast!
> The day of reckoning has come!
> (*Unable to control their anger, the villagers rush forward to beat* HUANG.)
> (*The district head and others stop them.*)

DISTRICT HEAD   Friends, don't beat him yet!   Let Hsi-erh finish.

HSI-ERH (*sings*):
> But Aunty Chang, she saved me,
> So I could leave the tigers' den.
> It was pitch black!

ALL (*sing*):
> *It was pitch black!*

HSI-ERH (*sings*):
> *And the way was dark!*

ALL (*sing*):
> *And the way was dark!*

HSI-ERH (*sings*):
> *I didn't know where to turn!*

ALL (*sing*):
> *Where did you go?*

HSI-ERH (*sings*):
> *I stayed in a cave in the mountain,*
> *Far from people and out of the sun,*
> *Eating raw fruit and offerings,*
> *Till I seemed neither ghost nor man!*
> *But I refused to die,*
> *Though stones rot or streams run dry!*
> *I bore my hardships till today,*
> *And today they have vanished away!*

WANG, CHANG and PEASANT WOMEN (*sing*):
> *In the light of the sun....*

HSI-ERH (*sings*):
> *Let vengeance be done!*

PEASANT WOMEN (*sing*):
> *She'll be avenged in the light of the sun!*

ALL (*sing*):
> *Now our time has come,*
> *We must be revenged!*
> *We want justice done,*
> *Hsi-erh must be avenged!*

(*No longer to be stopped they rush forward and beat* HUANG *and* MU.)

(*The district head and other cadres try to stop the crowd. The district head stands on a table.*)

DISTRICT HEAD (*shouts*) Friends! I represent the government. I support your charges against Land-

"She'll be avenged in the light of the sun!"

lord Huang. We will certainly avenge Hsi-erh.
First let us arrest Huang and Mu for public trial
according to proper legal procedure.

(*All cheer excitedly.*)

(*Members of the Self Defence Corps tie up*
HUANG *and* MU.)

ALL (*sing*):

> *Landlord Huang, you have bowed your head!*
> *You quake with dread!*
> *You have bowed your head!*
> *You quake with dread!*
> *Age-old feudal bonds*
> *Today are cut away!*
> *Crushing iron chains*
> *Will be smashed to bits today!*

(*The song is repeated.*)

(*The sun rises. It shines brightly on* HSI-ERH
and the surging crowd, who shout for joy and sing):

> *We, who suffered in days bygone,*
> *Shall be our own masters from now on!*
> *Shall be our own masters from now on!*
> *Our—own—masters—from—now—on!*

(LANDLORD HUANG *crouches before the crowd
like a felled tree.*)

(*The peasants stand proudly under the sun,
countless arms raised high.*)

(*CURTAIN*)

SONGS FROM
"THE WHITE-HAIRED GIRL"

THE NORTH WIND BLOWS

Pei fêng (na kê) ch'ui,   hsüeh hua (na kê) p'iao,
Tiehch'u mench'ü tuo chang   cheng ch'i (na kê) t'ien,

hsüeh hua (na kê) p'iao p'iao   nien lai   tao.
san shih (na kê) wan shang   huan mei hui huan.

Ta sheng tse kei lê   yü chiao tse

mien,   wo têng wo tê tieh tieh   hui chia kuo nien.

WAITING FOR DAD

Wo p'an tieh tieh

hsin chung chi, têng tieh hui lai hsin huan

hsi.   Tieh tieh tai hui pai mien lai, huan huan hsi hsi

kuo kê nien,   huan huan hsi hsi kuo kê nien.

RED RIBBON

Allegro

Jên chia tê kuei nü

yu hua tai, wo tieh ch'ien shao pu nēng mai, ch'ēh hui lai êrh ch'ih

hung t'ou shêng, kei wo tsa ch'ih lai. Ai!— tsa ya tsa ch'ih

lai.

The North Wind Blows

HSI-ERH (*sings*):

The north wind blows, the snow flakes whirl,
A flurry of snow brings in New Year.
Dad's been hiding a week because of his debt,
Though it's New Year's Eve, he's still not back.
Aunty's given me maize flour, and I'm waiting
For Dad to come home and spend New Year.

Waiting for Dad

HSI-ERH (*sings*):

I feel so restless waiting for Dad,
But when he comes home I'll be happy.
He'll bring some white flour back with him,
And we'll have a really happy New Year!

Red Ribbon

HSI-ERH (*sings*):

Other girls have flowers to wear,
But Dad can't afford to buy flowers;
So he's bought two feet of red ribbon
For me to tie in my hair!